Real life, real answers.
_____
Your will and estate planning

Real life, real answers.

Your will and estate planning

by
Fred Tillman &
Susan G. Parker

Houghton Mifflin Company   Boston
1990

For information about permission to reproduce selections from this book, write to
Permissions, Houghton Mifflin Company, 2 Park Street, Boston, Massachusetts
02108.

Library of Congress Catalog Card Number: 89-85915
ISBN: 0-395-51094-5

General editors: Barbara Binswanger, James Charlton, Lee Simmons

Design by Hudson Studio

"Real life, real answers" is a trademark of the John Hancock Mutual Life Insurance
Company.

Printed in the United States of America

10 9 8 7 6 5 4 3 2 1

Although this book is designed to provide accurate and authoritative information in
regard to the subject matter covered, neither the authors and general editors nor the
publisher are engaged in rendering legal, accounting, or other professional service.
If legal advice or other expert assistance is required, the services of a competent
professional should be sought.

Contents

Introduction

True, you can't take it with you;
but then, that's not the place where it
comes in handy.
                    —Brendan Francis

For an Egyptian king, estate planning meant building a great pyramid and filling it with all his possessions. The goal was to have them available in the next life so he could "live" comfortably. The pyramid was the key estate planning tool. It provided the bridge for the transfer of assets upon death.

Today we're also concerned about transferring our assets upon death, but our focus is not on what we'll be taking with us. Even people who look forward to a next life are pretty sure they won't be taking their cars, bank accounts, homes, or mortgage payments with them. But what will happen to your assets? And will they be sufficient to provide for loved ones?

Arranging for the accumulation, conservation, and transfer of your assets is estate planning. While putting all of one's earthly possessions in pyramid storage may have its appeal, people today generally want to decide who will get their wealth when they're gone. They also want to protect against a certain uncle in Washington, D.C., from getting too much.

What it boils down to is, who will get what and how will they get it? The other fundamental part of any reasonable estate plan is to ensure that you live comfortably in the meanwhile.

You are ready to begin planning your estate if you've got some things of value that you want to pass on, and if there are people in your life, most likely your family, that you want to pass them on to.

Whether that day is a month from now, a year from now, or another 50 years from now, there's one thing that's certain. You'd rather pass on your wealth to the important people in your life than to Uncle Sam. The federal estate and gift tax "unified credit" will shield up to $600,000 in assets from federal taxes. With a top estate tax rate of 55 percent, it is reassuring to know that most of us can eliminate taxes on even larger estates by taking the right steps now.

Estate planning involves much more than just avoiding taxes, however. Each chapter of this book will cover another important building block. You'll learn how to make an accounting of your assets; why you may want to change the way you hold title to certain property; the role of insurance in providing for your loved ones; and the types of things that should be covered in your will. You'll look into the probate process and the pros and cons of avoiding it. Perhaps most important, you'll get an idea of what you can do on your own, and what tasks are best left to professionals.

You will need help beyond this book. It is possible to plan your estate and make out a legally enforceable will without using an attorney. Don't! The risks are too great. Using this book will help you cut costs; it lays the groundwork for the planning process and may reduce your attorney's bill.

Hundreds of years of laws, precedent, and tradition have created the awesome body of today's "legalese" in the areas of trusts and estates. This book dispenses with legalese. It presents stories, documents, and examples throughout in simplified language. They tend to generalize and leave out the precision needed in legal documents. Bear in mind that the forms in this book are *not* usable for legal purposes.

Whether you're married or single, have children or don't, are young or *not* so young, the information and strategies in this book are central to formulating your estate plan. Federal tax consequences, the use of insurance, and the value of a will are universal planning considerations. But these fundamentals are only part of the picture.

Each state has its own laws that may impact on your plan. Whether a will is properly drawn or whether an estate must be probated are determined under state law. Also, some states have estate taxes. Be mindful as you read this book that individual state laws are not addressed here.

Like an Egyptian king's pyramid, your estate plan is created block by block. This book sets out the blocks that most of us should consider. While not all the blocks will fit your situation, you'll learn what is important for a sound estate plan that meets your needs.

CHAPTER I

Getting started

M ark Twain once said that if you put all your eggs in one basket, watch that basket! This chapter takes a closer look at what's in your basket. It will help you look at the nature and extent of what you own and how you own it. You'll also take a look at your family situation and the beneficiaries that you'd like to provide for.

You'll review the estate planning apparatus that's already in place. Do you have a will? Does it need updating? These questions will lead to a consideration of the aspects of your estate planning that may require the assistance of a professional.

DO YOU NEED A WILL?

Consider Ron and Joan McFaul. They're a working couple with two small children. Their sole asset is a home they've just purchased. They took title jointly and know that, with this form of ownership, the survivor will end up as the sole owner of the home. Since the house is their only asset and the survivor will get it, both Ron and Joan think they don't have to worry about wills.

But what if they should die together, without wills? Will their children get the house? Maybe so. But who will get the kids? Assume that both Ron and Joan have a number of brothers and sisters. The children may be up for grabs. Would Ron and Joan have preferred to choose who would care for their children? Could they have made that choice?

The answer is yes. But this choice is usually covered in a will. A letter to whom it may concern may not be binding. You need a will to appoint a guardian. On a matter as important as this, you need to take action. And you need a lawyer to draft the will.

These are the types of issues that emerge as you start looking in your basket of assets and responsibilities. For Ron and Joan, the immediate concern may be to draft wills appointing a guardian. Their concerns may change as they acquire new assets, have more children, get divorced, or start second marriage. So today's plan may change as components in your life change. That's why you've got to *watch that basket*.

WHY PLAN YOUR ESTATE?

Quite simply, because if you don't plan how your estate will be divided, someone else will divide it for you. What we're talking about here are state laws of intestacy. "Intestacy" refers to dying without a will. The individual states have enacted these laws to provide for the passing of property in the way lawmakers think most people would have wanted. The goal is usually to divide the estate among the closest blood relatives. For a married person who dies with children, the estate may be divided between the surviving spouse and kids. If you have children, it's unlikely that your spouse will inherit everything. The estate of a single person would generally pass to parents and siblings.

For some, the state's judgment may be fine. For Maggie and Ted Enders, it wasn't. Maggie and Ted had been married 18 years when Ted suddenly passed away. The couple had no children and had lived comfortably. All of their property, their condominium, two cars, and vacation home were in Ted's name. Things ended up that way because he'd taken a more active role in managing the couple's affairs. He was in good health and never bothered to make a will. He always figured Maggie would get everything when he died.

But Maggie got only half his estate. Ted's parents got the other half. Why? Since Ted had no will, the property passed in accordance with the state's intestacy laws. Whether Ted was close to his parents or not, he expected his wife would end up with the estate. So did she. State intestacy laws fill in the blanks when you don't.

AVOIDING ESTATE TAXES

When you decide who will get your estate, you also decide who won't. The beneficiary most estate planners want to cut out is Uncle Sam. While many believe that there's nothing certain but death and taxes, smart planners know estate taxes can be avoided and in most cases eliminated entirely.

Let's look at Fred and Ellen Jackson, a couple approaching retirement with grown children. They own a substantially appreciated home in the suburbs of Boston and a second home in Florida. Fred is retiring in a few years and is fully vested with significant retirement benefits. Ellen's only asset is a half-interest in the family home. They each have wills, drafted years ago, leaving all their property to each other, with the remainder to the kids.

Fred dies five years down the road, after receiving a $750,000 lump sum retirement plan payout. This, together with his other assets, yields an estate worth $1.5 million, all of which passes to his wife. His estate pays no federal estate tax because there's an unlimited marital deduction. This deduction allows you to leave everything you own to a spouse and not pay a dime in estate taxes. But when Ellen dies four years later there's a tax disaster!

Since she was a widow, Ellen's estate could not take advantage of the unlimited marital deduction. Part of her assets ($600,000) are shielded from estate tax because of the so-called "unified credit." This credit works like a personal exemption and lets everyone pass up to $600,000 in gifts and/or estate assets tax-free. But a big chunk of the remaining assets, which had appreciated since the time of her husband's death, was needlessly lost to taxes.

We're not talking about a couple of dollars either. If Ellen's estate was worth $2 million, the tax bill would be $588,000. This result could have been avoided through planning.

PLANNING MEANS HAVING IT YOUR WAY

A third reason for planning your estate is to make sure that your wishes are carried out. Most people want to ensure an orderly transition in their family affairs upon their death. For example, you may be a single parent with an absent former spouse; you want to be sure the kids will have a home and funds. You may have an elderly parent living with you who would be without a home or support upon your passing. Teenagers may have to be put through college and you want to make sure these costs are covered if you're not around to pay the bills.

You may want to provide for children from a prior marriage while providing for a current spouse. Or maybe you've been living with someone for years and are not married. You may want that person to get your wealth or you may want to prevent that result.

Special issues arise in connection with business interests as well. You may own a share in a business that you'd like to pass on to your family, but your partners would rather not have your wife and kids as partners. They'd rather buy out your interest if you're not around. Maybe you'd like to pass a family business to the one child who's worked in it with you and yet still provide adequately for the rest of your family.

These are just a few examples of the kind of loose ends that you can and should tie up by planning your estate. In fact these loose ends are often the core around which you build your estate plan.

WHAT ARE YOU WORTH?

What you have, less what you owe, is what you're worth. You've got the job of figuring this out. The asset checklist on pages 16 to 17 can be your road map for determining your net worth. It should be reviewed periodically—at least once a year—to give you an idea of where you're headed with respect to financial security for your retirement and for your beneficiaries.

It's a good idea to assemble your important documents so that things are in order for your family. These papers would include real estate deeds, stock certificates, employment contracts, divorce decrees, business agreements, bank accounts, and insurance policies. They, too, should be reviewed periodically to be sure they are in order and do not require updating. For example, your insurance needs may change as you acquire more assets or as your dependents grow in number. A document checklist is included on page 11 to get you started.

The nature of your assets will impact on your estate plan. For example, you'll want your estate to have liquid funds to provide for your family during the period your estate is being handled, not to mention the funds needed to pay for executor's fees, administrative costs, and taxes, if any. If you leave a working business interest to a child, cash may be needed to foot the estate tax bill on that interest. The last thing you want is for the child to have to sell the business because there's no money to pay the taxes.

How to value assets

Two pointers are in order about figuring value. The first concerns how to value things. For some assets, that's easy. The amount invested in a CD is pretty certain, with minor variations depending on accrued interest. The value of stocks and bonds can be found in the newspaper's financial section and valued as of a particular day. With a car you might refer to a "blue book" (available in most libraries) for its trade-in value. For many tangible assets you can look at comparable items and figure out value. But for one-of-a-kind things, determining value is more difficult.

If you've ever tried to sell a home and asked brokers to give you an idea about a suitable selling price, you're familiar with the problem: For every broker there's a different price. If your assets include real estate, closely held business interests, art work, or significant jewelry, you may need input from an expert appraiser.

Though you might be inclined to stick with your best guesstimate, too much may be at stake to rely on that alone. Reason: When a federal estate tax return is filed, the value of all property is listed on the return, even if no tax is due. Let's say the unified credit and the unlimited marital deduction do not wipe out your estate tax bill. Your executor's goal will be to keep the value of assets low, to keep taxes at a minimum. The IRS, on the other hand, has an interest in valuing things on the high side to collect more taxes.

In other situations, even if no tax is due, the IRS will have an incentive to challenge the value. For example, if you own a large asset that you leave to your spouse, it will avoid tax because of the marital deduction. But chances are it may end up in your spouse's estate. The way the property is valued in the estate of the first to die may impact on the value in the second estate, when it will no longer be shielded from tax by the unlimited marital deduction. If you've been assessing value on hunches and guesswork, you may just be postponing the day of reckoning.

The other thing to keep in mind concerning value is how much of something you own. Generally, it is only that portion of something you own that is included in your estate. For example, if you own a one-third interest in a partnership, only one-third of the partnership will be included in your estate. But as you'll see in the next section, with certain types of property, your interest may be different than you'd expect.

FORMS OF OWNERSHIP AND PROPERTY INTERESTS

Being able to use, control, and dispose of property is what being an owner is about. With respect to real property—land, homes, buildings, and the like—ownership is proved by having the deed or title to the property registered in your name. The same is generally true for stocks, bonds, and other financial instruments. But for property owned jointly, how title is taken can be critical.

Jointly owned property

There are three types of joint ownership that you should know about. The first is called a *tenancy in common.* If Al and Sue buy a house in the country, and each wants to own 50 percent of the property independent of the other, they should take title as tenants in common. This way each owner can sell or bequeath (leave to a beneficiary under a will) his or her share, and is responsible only for that proportionate share of taxes and expenses.

If Al and Sue rent out the house, each would get half the rental income and be responsible for paying half the expenses. If Sue decided to sell her interest to Mary, Al would have Mary as a co-owner. Sue would be entitled to sell her interest. If Al died owning the interest in the house as a tenant in common, 50 percent of the value of the property would be included in his estate. Under his will, Al could leave his 50 percent share to anyone he wishes. It doesn't automatically go to Sue.

The other two forms of joint ownership, a *joint tenancy with right of survivorship* and a *tenancy by the entirety,* work differently. They both carry the right of survivorship. Each owner's interest automatically passes to the survivor. For example, if Al dies owning an interest in the house as a joint tenant, his interest comes to an end and Sue becomes the sole owner of the entire property. What's more, the entire value of the property will be

DOCUMENT CHECKLIST

- ☐ Birth certificate
- ☐ Marriage certificate
- ☐ Antenuptial agreements
- ☐ Postnuptial agreements
- ☐ Divorce decrees
- ☐ Separation agreements
- ☐ List of heirs
- ☐ Military service record
- ☐ Social Security card
- ☐ Medical records
- ☐ Will, original
- ☐ Will, copy
- ☐ Previous wills
- ☐ Spouse's will
- ☐ Tax records
- ☐ Life insurance policies
- ☐ General insurance policies
- ☐ Stock certificates
- ☐ Bonds
- ☐ Notes receivable
- ☐ Mortgages receivable
- ☐ Deeds
- ☐ Leases
- ☐ Estate inventory
- ☐ Bank books
- ☐ Financial records
- ☐ Business agreements and records
- ☐ Trust instruments
- ☐ Location/keys for safe deposit box
- ☐ Cemetery deeds
- ☐ Employee benefit plan statements
- ☐ Directions regarding burial

---

included in Al's estate unless the estate can prove Sue's actual contribution to the purchase or improvement of the property.

A tenancy by the entirety is the same as a joint tenancy in that it carries a right of survivorship. The big difference is that, by definition, only a husband and wife can hold property in this form. If Al and Sue are husband and wife and own the house as tenants by the entirety, when Al dies, Sue becomes the sole owner. But the estate tax kicker is that only 50 percent of the property's value will be included in his estate. With a spouse you do not have to prove who paid what. Only half the value of jointly held property is included for tax purposes.

These forms of joint ownership are also treated differently when it comes to probate (covered in Chapter VII; probate is the process of carrying out the wishes expressed in your will with court supervision). If Al owns the country home as a tenant in common, his will can provide that his best friend Jay inherit his interest. The property must go through probate for title to be transferred to Jay. If Al dies owning the property as a joint tenant or tenant by the entirety, probate will not be required to transfer title to Sue.

Community property

Spouses get special treatment under the tax law. As you can see from the previous examples, each spouse is presumed to own 50 percent of property held as a tenant by the entirety. Other joint owners have to prove their contribution to limit the inclusion of only 50 percent of jointly held property in their estates. This policy of assuming that property acquired during marriage is half owned by each spouse is built into the laws of some states and is referred to as "community property."

Under the laws of Arizona, California, Idaho, Louisiana, Nevada, New Mexico, Texas, and Washington, property acquired during marriage, other than by gift or inheritance, is deemed owned equally by each spouse. Wisconsin law also has community property characteristics. Should you die while married and living in one of these states, only half of the community property would be included in your estate. If you are married and acquire property in a community property state, and then move to a non–community property state, the property will generally remain equally owned by each spouse. Community property laws may affect what you can do with certain property and may create special planning considerations.

Property interests measured by time

In the examples above involving joint ownership, both owners enjoy their ownership rights at the same time. But there are other property interests in which people have successive rights in the same property. A common example is a lease. If you rent an apartment, the building's owner gives you the right to use the apartment in accordance with the terms of your lease. The prior tenant had rights before you moved in, and at the end of your lease term or rental period, someone else may take over the apartment. A lease is a limited type of property right transferred for a fixed period of time.

In other cases, the fixed term may be based on your life or

the life of someone else. For example, an annuity may promise a steady monthly income until your death. With a joint and survivor annuity, the surviving spouse continues to receive an annuity after the first spouse dies. Such an annuity may provide the surviving spouse with income for a fixed period—say 20 years. The death of the first spouse becomes the measuring rod for the 20-year period.

The time line

Ownership is frequently divided into periods along a time line. How does this work? Consider Grandma Jenny. She has a big old house which she gives to her son Adam. However, as part of the deal, she tells Adam he can own it only for his lifetime. When he dies, her grandson Scott gets the house.

Grandma Jenny owned the entire bundle of property rights in the house—the right to use the house today and to give, sell, or bequeath it under her will. What she gave to Adam was less than what she owned. Adam received the right to use it for his lifetime. This type of interest is called a "present interest" or "life estate" because Adam can enjoy it now but only "owns" the property until his death. He can't give, sell, or bequeath it because at his death it belongs to Scott.

What Grandma Jenny gave to her grandson is called a "remainder." Since Scott's rights come into play only later, he has what is called a "future interest." However, when Adam dies and Scott gets the property, Scott will have the entire bundle of property rights in the house. He can sell it, give it away, or leave it to someone under his will.

Cutting the pie another way

Another way to divide an ownership interest is illustrated with property transferred into a trust. Assume that Grandma Jenny kept her big old house and instead put all her stocks and bonds into a trust. She wants Adam to get all the income that the trust funds generate. When Adam dies, she wants her grandson

Scott to get all the stocks and bonds. Adam's right to receive all the income from the trust is called an "income interest." Scott's right to get the stocks and bonds when his father dies is another form of remainder interest. Scott will get the whole bundle of rights with respect to the stocks and bonds that make up the trust principal. His interest will not be limited to only the income produced by those assets.

Whether something is a present or future interest affects both its value and how it's treated for tax purposes.

PROFESSIONAL EXPERTISE

Estate planning can make use of the expertise of a lot of different professionals. It can involve accountants, appraisers, bankers, financial planners, insurance people, investment advisers, and, of course, lawyers. Within the field of law, there are lawyers who specialize in tax, trusts and estates, and property. How much expert advice do you need?

Certain things can and should be done on your own, such as figuring out what you own and what you want to do with your wealth. This will save you a lot in the long run. While experts can implement the mechanics, the choices are really up to you.

After you've taken a hard look at these areas, you may conclude that things are generally in order. Maybe only a new will or a new investment strategy is needed. Then at least you've narrowed the field of advisers who can help you.

If your estate is large and property interests or family entanglements are complex, it may seem that you need most of the professional services mentioned above. If it's hard to know where to go first, take it one step at a time. You're best off seeking a captain for the team—a person who can orchestrate your plan even if he or she cannot perform each task personally. That person can then assist you in selecting other advisers that may be needed.

If you have an adviser such as an accountant or lawyer

whom you have faith in, that person would be a good starting point. The second best route to good advice is to ask friends or colleagues for recommendations.

Here are a few pointers to start you on your way:

Does the adviser have a professional designation? Lawyers are licensed (that is, admitted to the bar) in the state in which they practice. Other planners are certified by respective licensing or professional associations. For example, accountants who are certified by state licensing authorities are certified public accountants. Certified Financial Planners (CFP) and Chartered Life Underwriters (CLU) are certified by professional organizations.

Does your prospective planner really know estate planning? You may ask how you'll be able to determine this. Actually this book will increase your knowledge and you will be in a better position to assess the planner. Not every attorney is an expert in this field, nor is every accountant. A jack of all trades, even one who holds a professional license, may not be your best choice.

Is the planner looking out for your interests or more interested in a sale? Many planners also work at selling investment products. Often it may be difficult to assess who's helping whom. That doesn't mean such planners cannot be trusted, but you should certainly be aware of possible conflicts of interest if you're combining your estate planning with someone else's livelihood.

Don't forget your common sense! While it's important to assess the experience and expertise of a potential planner, all the diplomas, certifications, and the like won't be worth much if you feel uneasy about how the process is being conducted.

ASSET CHECKLIST

Date_____

(update at least once a year)

	Type of ownership (husband/wife/joint)	Fair market value

ASSETS:

Cash

Checking/savings accounts	_____	$ _____
Money market funds/CDs	_____	_____
Cash management account	_____	_____
Credit union account	_____	_____
Life insurance cash values	_____	_____
Total cash assets		$ _____

Marketable investments

Common and preferred stocks	_____	$ _____
Corporate bonds	_____	_____
Municipal bonds	_____	_____
Mutual funds	_____	_____
Other	_____	_____
Total marketable investments		$ _____

Real estate investments

Personal residence	_____	$ _____
Vacation/second home	_____	_____
Rental property	_____	_____
Real estate partnerships	_____	_____
Other	_____	_____
Total real estate investments		$ _____

Other investments

Business interests	_____	$ _____
Partnerships	_____	_____
Other	_____	_____
Total other investments		$ _____

Retirement

IRAs	_____	$ _____
Pension accounts	_____	_____
Profit sharing plan accounts	_____	_____
401(k) plan assets	_____	_____
Savings, bonus, or thrift plans	_____	_____
ESOP	_____	_____
Keogh plan	_____	_____
Deferred compensation	_____	_____
Supplemental retirement plans	_____	_____
Other	_____	_____
Total retirement assets		$ _____

	Type of ownership (husband/wife/joint)	Fair market value
Personal		
Cars	_____	$ _____
Boats/planes	_____	_____
Jewelry and furs	_____	_____
Collectibles	_____	_____
Art	_____	_____
Antiques	_____	_____
Household furnishings	_____	_____
Other	_____	_____
Total personal assets		$ _____
TOTAL ASSETS		$ _____

LIABILITIES:

Current		
Credit cards	_____	$ _____
Bank	_____	_____
Store	_____	_____
Other	_____	_____
Credit lines	_____	_____
Overdraft	_____	_____
Home equity lines	_____	_____
Unsecured credit line	_____	_____
Income taxes payable	_____	_____
Property taxes payable	_____	_____
Total current liabilities		$ _____

Long-term		
Home mortgage	_____	$ _____
Second mortgage	_____	_____
Mortgages on business property	_____	_____
Mortgages on investment property	_____	_____
Car loans	_____	_____
Tuition loans	_____	_____
Bank loans	_____	_____
Margin loans	_____	_____
Life insurance policy loans	_____	_____
Other	_____	_____
Total long-term liabilities		$ _____
TOTAL LIABILITIES		$ _____

NET WORTH (assets minus liabilities)		$ _____

CHAPTER II

Where there's a will...

F or many of us, estate planning really takes on meaning when we consider a last will and testament. It is often the only document that outlines the entire game plan—who gets what and how. At one time, a will disposed of personal property and a testament disposed of real property. Today it's all taken care of in one document.

Your will is a set of instructions to be followed by the person you pick to carry out the plans. That person is the executor if he's a man, and the executrix if she's a woman. Lawyers also have a name for you when you write a will. If you're a man, you become the testator; a woman is a testatrix.

But don't let this smattering of legalese fool you. Unless you're an expert at drafting your game plan, have a lawyer do it for you. He or she knows the nuances and state law ramifications. An attorney can question things you may have overlooked or not even considered.

He or she also adds legitimacy to the process in the event your sanity is ever called into question. No joke! Disgruntled relatives have been known to contest a will or two. If a lawyer oversees the proceeding, he or she can attest to your competency.

For some, only one will may be needed. You may have a long-term marriage, with a spouse and children who are the sole objects of your bounty. Your choices are clear and remain that way. For others, your will may change along with your marital situation. That's nothing to worry about because you can change your will as often as you like. In fact, your will *should* be reviewed periodically to make sure it addresses changed situations and still reflects your wishes.

WHAT A WILL LOOKS LIKE

Not everyone has the same favorite family heirloom, impeccably maintained antique car, or prized beer can collection, but the manner of passing such objects is pretty standard. Wills do vary with individual situations, but there's a commonly used format. Let's look at the will of Maxwell Addison:

Last Will and Testament
of
Maxwell Addison

I, Maxwell Addison, live at 123 Main Street, Anytown, Any State, and hereby make and declare this to by my will. I hereby revoke any and all wills and codicils previously made by me.

1. I am presently married to Tara Addison and have two children, Raymond and John.
2. I direct that my debts, funeral expenses, and taxes be paid out of my residuary estate and not be allocated or apportioned against any person's share.
3. I give my entire record collection to my brother Richard Addison, if he survives me.
4. I give the sum of $20,000 to my sister Lisa Addison if she survives me, and if she does not survive me, to her surviving children in equal shares.
5. I give all my stocks to Any State University.
6. I give the rest of my personal property to my wife Tara if she survives me.
7. I give any real property I own at my death to my wife Tara.
8. I give all the rest, residue, and remainder of my estate, both

real and personal, to my wife if she survives me, or if not, to my children in equal shares.

If, at the time of my death, a child of mine has passed away, that child's share shall pass to his children, if any. (In legal documents, the phrase *per stirpes* is used to confer this result.)

9. If at the time of my death any of my beneficiaries is under age 25, that beneficiary's share shall be held in trust, to be used for the benefit of that child. It shall be paid over to him when he is 25 years old.

10. I hereby appoint my wife Tara Addison to serve as my executrix and as trustee under any trust set up under my will. If she does not survive me, I appoint my sister Lisa Addison as the alternate executrix and as the guardian of my children Raymond and John.

Dated:

_____
Maxwell Addison

On this   day of   ,   , Maxwell Addison declared this to be his Last Will and Testament and asked us to witness his signature. We saw him sign his will, and believe him to be of sound mind and over the age of eighteen.

_____
Witness One

_____
Witness Two

STATE LAWS

Each state has its own rules regarding what it takes to have a valid will. Generally a person must be at least 18 years of age and of sound mind, and the will must be witnessed by two or three people.

Also, contrary to popular belief, you execute only one will at a time. A will is not a document you make in duplicate. Reason:

One way to revoke a will is to tear it up. If you execute a number of copies of the original (for example, one for your spouse and one for the vault) and then tear up only one, where do you stand? You stand in line for problems with probate.

BASIC FORMAT

Let's take a closer look at the layout of the will. Each paragraph generally discusses a new topic. Plus there are certain things that must be covered in a will, such as appointing a guardian. Maxwell Addison liked to think he was a wild and crazy guy. But let's see how standard his will is.

Openers

The opening clause identifies the writer and states where he or she lives. This is important for a couple of reasons. First, whether a will is valid is determined under state law. Second, state law may also affect how certain property interests pass and whether state death taxes are imposed on the estate.

The opening paragraph also revokes prior wills and codicils. (A codicil is an amendment to a will. It usually must be signed with the same formalities as a will.) The easiest way to get rid of an old will is to write a new one, revoking all prior wills. From the dates of signing, a court can tell which one is current.

Family status

This provision gives your executor an idea about your family relationships. This may have a bearing on who has to be notified of a probate proceeding and who the rightful beneficiaries are. For example, what happens if Maxwell Addison has another child before his death but never changes his will? Under some state laws, the will would be interpreted to include all of his children even though he refers only to Raymond and John. The same type of issue can arise in connection with a spouse.

By including a family status clause, it may be easier to discern your intention if a question arises later. For example, if

What is a right of election?

L et's say Maxwell Addison was not married at the time of his death, but his will makes provision for a spouse. Since the ex-spouse is no longer a spouse, gifts to her would lapse.

But assume that Maxwell was not married at the time he wrote the will, but was married at the time of his death. Would his wife be cut out of the will because he made no provision for her?

No! Under most state laws spouses can "elect" to receive a fixed portion of their deceased partner's estate. This portion is fixed by statute and expressed either as a percentage (for example, 10 percent) or fractional share (one-third) of the estate. The right of election can also be exercised if a spouse is cut out of a will or receives less than the elective share.

Maxwell had not provided for his wife in his will, it would be clear his intent was to exclude her. However, if he was not married at the time he wrote the will but later did marry and never changed it, a different situation would be presented.

Payment of debts and taxes

Your estate is going to be liable for debts and taxes whether or not you tell your executor to pay them. So, what is the purpose of this clause? It lets you decide which beneficiaries will foot the tax bill. If no provision is made, state law supplies the source for the tax money. Here Maxwell wants the debts and taxes to be paid out of the residuary, so the share to his wife will be cut back.

Bequests

Imagine you have a cartful of groceries to give away. You could start by giving away a can of Spam, then all the cold cereal, then a quarter of what's left in the cart, and then whatever else is left. The basket will be empty when you're through. That's exactly how the dispositive provisions of a will are written. The specific items are carved out first.

The record collection, or a can of Spam for that matter, would be a "specific bequest," that is, a specific item of personal property left to a specific person. If Maxwell's brother is not alive to receive the record collection, the collection would pass as part of the residuary.

The $20,000 cash to sister Lisa is called a "general bequest." The source of the $20,000 is not specified. The executrix will make the decisions regarding how this legacy will be paid.

If you want to bequeath each item you own to one of your 42 grandchildren, it's probably a good idea not to clutter up your will—particularly if you change your mind frequently. Each time you change your mind, you would have to write a new will, or at least a codicil. A better idea would be to have this information in a separate document that is entrusted to the most trustworthy of those grandchildren—the one who will see to it that your wishes are respected and carried out.

The bequest of stocks to Any State University is different. The source of the gift is certain, that is, "stocks." But the amount of the gift is uncertain until Maxwell's death. If Maxwell has sold all of his stocks before he dies, there will be no bequest to Any State U.

The disposition of personal property and real property (land, buildings, real estate) is often taken care of in separate paragraphs. One reason is that if you are married you will want your spouse to have your home, furnishings, the car, etc. A specific bequest of this property ensures that these items will not wind up in the residuary, where they may be disposed of to take care of other legacies.

The residuary

Finally and fittingly comes the residue. Whatever's left in the cart, after debts and taxes and all the bequests in the paragraphs above, goes to Maxwell's wife. In real life, the residuary is an important source of tax and administrative monies that may be needed through the estate administration process. The share going to residuary beneficiaries may be reduced by these amounts.

Creation of a trust

Trusts are set up under wills for a variety of reasons, many of which are discussed in the chapters ahead. For example, a trust may be created to provide for a surviving spouse or to receive life insurance proceeds payable at your death. A trust is frequently set up under a will to hold property for any beneficiary who is a minor.

Selecting executors, trustees, and guardians

A variety of fiduciaries are also appointed under a will. Here Maxwell names his executrix, trustee, and guardian. He also names an alternate. The clause might also provide for the waiving or posting of a bond by the fiduciary and the compensation to be paid.

It goes without saying that the persons selected for these roles should be chosen with care. Depending on your situation, the job may be complex or simple and may involve nasty family politics. Just because you trust a spouse, sibling, or close friend does not mean that person is up to the task of handling an estate. Many executors hire professionals to actually take care of the estate administration.

State laws usually prescribe standard powers your executor and trustee can exercise regarding the management and investment of assets. You can change or enlarge on these powers by including clauses to that effect in the will or trust provisions. For example, you could enable your executor to retain a large block of closely held stock that does not pay a dividend, even though state law may impose different investment standards. You can also give your fiduciaries the right to consult or hire outside experts, at the expense of your estate.

Fiduciary fees

E xecutors are entitled to fees unless they are waived. They are also required to post a bond. In many states fees are fixed by law and range from 2 to 5 percent of the probate estate. Sometimes a "reasonable compensation" standard is used. If you're considering using a professional fiduciary, such as a bank or trust company, it's a good idea to know what reasonable compensation means to them. Also, some states set no fees at all and the sky may be the limit unless you provide otherwise by agreement. Fiduciary fees may be an important factor in determining the cash requirements of your estate.

WHAT CAN'T BE COVERED

Your will may have no effect on the disposition of certain types of assets. These include life insurance; retirement plan proceeds; jointly owned property with a right of survivorship; and property that is already out of your control, for example in an irrevocable trust.

These assets are also cut out of the probate process (see Chapter VII). Why? Because the property is already going to someone in accordance with a document you signed. Your wishes cannot be changed by your will.

Life insurance

When you take out insurance, you usually name a specific beneficiary. Let's say Maxwell Addison had insurance and named his brother Richard as the beneficiary. After he married Tara, he decided to leave the policy to her. Instead of notifying the insurance company, he changed his will to say "I leave the death proceeds of my Suburban Life Insurance policy to my wife Tara, not my brother Richard." What result? Tough luck, Tara.

Retirement plan proceeds

For many people today, whether they work in a Fortune 500

company, a closely held business, or somewhere in between, retirement benefits and deferred compensation can be substantial. These benefits are paid out of plans that take a variety of forms, including "qualified" retirement, profit sharing, or 401(k) plans; employee stock ownership plans (ESOPs); thrift plans; and savings and stock bonus plans. If you are self-employed, these plans may be referred to as HR-10 or Keogh plans.

Benefits from these plans, as well as monies payable from your individual retirement accounts (IRAs), are usually paid out in accordance with plan provisions. Also, plan participants frequently complete beneficiary designation forms. Special tax rules also come into play here. For example, married participants often must take their pension benefits in the form of a joint and survivor annuity, unless the spouse consents in writing to another form of benefit payout.

The important point here is that if these funds go to designated beneficiaries, per the plan rules and/or tax rules, your will cannot override the designation. In cases where it is possible to name your estate as the designated beneficiary, you can pass these assets per instructions under your will.

Jointly owned property with right of survivorship

If you own property with your spouse as a tenant by the entirety, or jointly own any property with another person with a right of survivorship, at your death your interest is extinguished. Gone, finito, kaput. There is nothing left for you to pass on under the terms of your will. The survivor gets all.

Maxwell Addison and his sister Lisa own a beach house as joint tenants with right of survivorship. At the time they purchased the home, both were single. Now each is married with a couple of kids. If Maxwell dies, Lisa will own the beach house. Maxwell's family gets nothing. If Lisa dies first, her kids and spouse are cut out.

In light of the changed circumstances, Maxwell and Lisa

could convert their ownership into a tenancy in common. With a tenancy in common, each co-owner can make a gift of his share of the property either during his or her lifetime, or under the will. Maxwell and Lisa could then bequeath their separate interests in the home to their respective heirs. If Maxwell dies, his family may still want to own the house with his sister. If not, they could sell out to her, or the entire property could be sold. Then Maxwell's heirs and Lisa will get their fair shares.

In short, Maxwell and Lisa must change the form of ownership to change how the property will pass. Maxwell can't just write a provision in his will leaving his share in the home to his wife and children. It won't work.

Property you no longer own

This may sound obvious, but for those who engage in wishful thinking it may not be. Your will cannot get back property you no longer own to give to someone else.

Let's look at Maxwell Addison again. Years ago Maxwell was addicted to a very insecure girl named Drizella who convinced him to set up an irrevocable trust for her. She was concerned that he would no longer love her when she was old and gray. Being young and in love he thought that day would never come.

To prove his love, Maxwell eagerly set up an irrevocable trust. Its only asset was title to the home the couple shared. Drizella is the sole beneficiary of this trust. To make a long story short, Maxwell has come to regret this early flight of fancy. He sometimes deludes himself into thinking he'll leave the home to his children under his will. Such a bequest will be meaningless, since he no longer owns the home.

CHAPTER III

Trusts are easy

A trust agreement can work with your will to round out your estate plans. Creating a trust enables you to set aside your assets or property as a separate pool to be managed and distributed according to your wishes by a trustee. Trusts can come into play while you're alive or upon your death.

Trusts that are written into your will to take effect when you die are called *testamentary trusts*. Trusts that go into effect while you're alive are called *inter vivos trusts*.

Both types of trusts can have the same provisions. It's just how they're set up that's different. Some trusts are designed to produce a tax benefit. Others accomplish different goals. They have a variety of uses and, as you'll see, they're not just for the rich.

WHAT A TRUST CAN DO FOR YOU

A trust is a contract between you and another person called the trustee. The contract provides that you give property to the trustee, who will hold it and/or distribute it in accordance with the terms of the contract. The terms of the contract are your wishes.

Trusts are set up for a variety of purposes. Therefore they contain a variety of terms. Some trusts also have the added advantage of favorable tax consequences. The transfer of property to a trust may be a gift and may therefore create a gift tax liability. Thereafter any income taxes may be payable by the trust itself or the ultimate beneficiaries.

Real life, real answers.

J erry Endrizzi is a widower who owns and runs a hardware store with two of his three kids. The third child has no interest in the business and is happily settled in a different career. Jerry wants to leave the business to the two kids who work in it. He's confident they will have a steady life income from the business, or a substantial asset they can sell down the road. He wants to provide the same level of comfort and security for his third child. He decides to place his remaining assets in trust, with his third child as sole beneficiary. He has selected a trustee to manage the assets, to assure a steady income stream to the child until such time as he feels the child will be capable of responsibly handling the assets himself.

Throughout this book you'll see many different reasons why people set up trusts. But the common denominator is usually to provide for the management, conservation, and flow of assets to someone you'd like to benefit.

ADVANTAGES TO PUTTING PROPERTY IN TRUST

There are several advantages to setting up an inter vivos trust, that is, making a gift of property in trust while you're still alive. First, even if the trust is revocable, the property in trust will avoid probate and challenges to your will. And it can ensure the uninterrupted flow of funds to your family in the event of your death or incapacity. If the trust is irrevocable, added pluses include getting assets out of your probate estate and avoiding estate tax on asset appreciation.

The reasons for setting up a testamentary trust, that is, a trust that comes into being at your death, are different. A chief goal here is to ensure constancy in management and administration of your assets, particularly assets such as life insurance and retirement benefits that do not come into being until after your death. Testamentary trusts are frequently set up to receive and distribute these assets.

TRUST BASICS

A simple trust can indeed be very simple. Property is transferred to a trust, a trustee is named, and he or she is told how to distribute income earned on the trust fund and the fund itself. Other standard provisions like fees and replacement trustees are also covered. State laws usually list the powers that a trustee can exercise, like buying and selling stock. You are free to add or subtract from the standard list as you see fit. Here's an example of a simple trust:

Thomas Miller
Simple Trust

I, Thomas Miller, hereby create the Thomas Miller Trust. I give up all right to alter, amend, or revoke this trust. I appoint the Surething Trust Company as trustee and am transferring 1,000 shares of Gadget stock, to be held in trust and used as follows:

1. During my life, the trustee shall pay all dividends and any other earnings on the trust assets to my daughter Anna.

2. At my death, the trustee shall distribute all the trust assets to my daughter Anna.

3. If Anna shall die while this property is still in trust, the trustee shall distribute the stock in equal shares to her children, if any. If none, the trustee shall distribute the assets to Any State University.

4. Surething Trust Company shall receive 5 percent of the trust earnings annually (paid out of the earnings) as its fee. Surething may exercise any and all of the statutory fiduciary powers. In addition, if the dividend on Gadget stock yields less than 5 percent of today's value, the trustee can sell the stock and reinvest the proceeds in higher yield investments.

_____

Thomas Miller

_____

Surething Trust Company
as "Trustee"

Since Tom gave up all rights to amend, alter, or revoke the trust, the stock is completely out of his control. Therefore he has made a gift of the 1,000 shares of stock. The Thomas Miller Trust will be a separate taxpayer, and Anna will have taxable income when she receives distributions from the trust.

If Tom had kept the right to revoke, alter, or amend the trust, or retained significant ownership rights, then he would be treated as the owner of the trust. For example, if Gadget Inc. was a closely held company and Tom gave up the right to revoke the trust but kept the voting rights on the stock, he'd be considered the owner of the stock.

Flexiblility

Different clauses can be added to accomplish different purposes. Since trusts may last for a long time, flexibility is the key. You want the trust to be able to handle changed circumstances. If the trust is revocable, you can always make changes. Even if it is irrevocable, you can give the trustee the power to make changes.

Power to "sprinkle"

A trustee or even the beneficiary can be given the power to invade principal for special needs. Income can be paid or "sprinkled" to several beneficiaries, on an as-needed basis. A sprinkling clause allows the trustee to make unequal payments to the various beneficiaries.

Let's say you've got two kids. You put assets in trust with the idea of using the funds to pay for their education. Now one is in college and the other is in high school. The trustee could use more of the trust income for the child in college to offset college expenses. Then when the second child is in college, more of the income can be used for him or her. These provisions, including when the sprinkle power should be cut off and assets distributed, should be considered carefully.

Real life, real answers.

S tanley and Edna Kaylor have a handicapped child who will never be self-supporting. They are fortunate in having good health and ample resources, but are concerned about who will take over financial responsibility for the child when they're gone. They create a special trust for this purpose. They want to be sure that the trust is properly drawn so that their child will not lose out on any other benefits she is entitled to under special programs.

Power to get trust principal

Another popular power given trustees is the right to use principal for the benefit of a beneficiary. The trustee is given the power to dip into the funds if the health, education, or support needs of the beneficiary require it. Sometimes this right to dip into principal is only allowed if the beneficiary has no other funds available. A right to use principal usually is not given to allow offspring to live better than you did.

Beneficiary's right to withdraw funds

You may want to give your beneficiaries the right to draw on the principal without requiring the trustee's permission. If the withdrawal right is unrestricted, the beneficiary will be deemed the owner of the trust. This withdrawal right is usually limited to the greater of $5,000 or 5 percent of the trust principal in a year, to avoid having the entire trust principal included in the beneficiary's estate when he or she dies.

REVOCABLE LIVING TRUSTS: AN ALTERNATIVE

A revocable living trust is essentially a hybrid between a will and a trust. How? You transfer the bulk of your assets into the trust and, in most states, you can be the trustee and manage the assets while you're alive. The trust document outlines the rules for managing and distributing the property at your death. Living trusts have become extremely popular. Let's look at some of the reasons.

If you choose to have a living trust as the main way to pass your assets, there are several advantages over a will. First, a will must be probated, with attendant legal fees, court costs, and matters open to the public eye (this is more fully covered in Chapter VII). Not so with a living trust. It avoids probate because it is not a bequest made under your will. But it can still pass property to the same beneficiaries at your death.

A big selling feature to some is that, in some states, you can be your own trustee. This means no management costs while you're alive, if you choose to avoid them. Even in a state where you cannot be your own trustee, a spouse or trusted relative can serve for no fee. At your death, or if you become mentally disabled, a successor trustee takes over. That person, be it a bank, friend, or relative, will distribute your assets or hold them in further trust, per your wishes.

At first glance you may think that a living trust accomplishes the same thing as a trust created under your will: It primarily kicks in after you kick off. That's true to some extent, but there's a big difference. Since a testamentary trust is part of your will, it goes through probate. Even if the two trusts contained identical provisions, the probate route may be much more costly.

How can you "fund" a living trust? In other words, what can you transfer to a living trust? Essentially anything you own. This includes title to real estate, marketable securities, and other investments. Let's assume our friend Maxwell Addison transfers some stock into a living trust. Here's what it looks like.

Maxwell Addison
Revocable Living Trust

I, Maxwell Addison, hereby create the Maxwell Addison Revocable Living Trust. It shall be funded with the shares of stock listed on the attached schedule. I name myself as trustee.

I reserve the right to revoke, amend, or alter this trust at any time.

The income and principal of this trust shall be distributed per my directions while I am alive. If I become incompetent, the successor trustee shall use the income and principal for myself and my family.

At my death, I direct my successor trustee to hold and distribute the trust's assets as follows:

1. If my wife shall survive me, the trustee shall pay all of the income in the trust to her for her life.

2. Upon her death, or if she is not alive at my death, I direct the trustee to use the trust assets for my children as follows:

   a. If any of my children is under the age of 21 when I die, all of the income of the trust shall be applied to that child's health, maintenance, education, and comfort.

   b. My trustee can also use the trust principal for the benefit of any child, if needed for emergencies or especially large expenses. If payments of principal are made, they need not be made in equal amounts, nor will they be charged against that child's ultimate share of trust assets.

   c. When my youngest child turns 21, the trust will be split into two subtrusts, one for each. The trustee shall pay each child the income from his subtrust. The trustee may draw upon the principal in the subtrust for emergencies or especially large expenses.

   d. When each child turns 30, my trustee shall distribute the remaining assets in the subtrust to him. If a child dies during the term of the trust, his share shall go to his children, if any; or, if none, it shall be divided into equal shares for my surviving children.

3. I appoint my brother Richard Addison as successor trustee. If he shall not serve for any reason, I appoint the Surething Trust Company as successor. My brother has agreed to serve as trustee without receiving a fee. If Surething Trust Company serves as trustee, it shall be entitled to compensation at the statutory rate.

_____

Maxwell Addison

What does it cost?

You'll need a lawyer to set up the trust and there may be some fees in connection with changing title to assets transferred to the trust. If you or a relative or friend serves as trustee, there should be no trustee fees. If you opt for a professional trustee, fees will depend on the state you live in and the types of assets to be held in trust.

These fees generally should be lower than probate costs on the same assets. Probate fees can average 4 to 7 percent of the gross value of an estate. Also, special higher fees come into play if assets are sold during the course of probate.

If any real estate, including your home or investment property, is transferred to the trust, there may be other costs. Fees are charged for changing title documents and recording new ones. Also, if the property has been financed or will be used as collateral, be sure to check with your lender. Many lenders won't get involved with financing on assets held by a revocable living trust.

Added bonus

As people get older, mental infirmity or illness can end their ability to manage their assets. A living trust is the primary way to ensure your property can be used for your benefit and then pass per your wishes. In a living trust you can name the individual you'd like to take over if you become incompetent.

You get to pick someone you can count on and your assets will be protected against unscrupulous relatives, friends, lovers,

Real life, real answers.

A rnie and Sadie Meyers have a great relationship. He loves to make money and control the finances and she's glad to have someone else do it. Arnie adores Sadie and plans to leave his estate to her when he's gone. But he's concerned that her greedy children from her first marriage or a fast-talking broker will take advantage of her. He leaves his legacy to her in trust to insure even cash flow and a comfortable lifestyle for her. She won't have to worry about having to say no to her children or the brokers who woo her, because she'll have no power to say yes.

or life-care schemes. A living trust may avoid the need to have a court appoint a conservator, that is, someone to manage your assets and affairs if you become mentally disabled. More important, there is no other document that allows you to provide for this contingency.

Keeping the right to revoke

Though living trusts can be revocable or irrevocable, there's greater flexibility in being able to change your mind. With a revocable trust you are free to swap assets, for example, to sell your home, keep the income, and keep up with changing situations. If you want the trust to be a will substitute, keep it as flexible as possible. If you are the trustee, you can allocate the benefits among family members in any way you see fit. Just keep your powers as trustee broad.

If the trust is irrevocable, the big benefit is having the asset appreciation removed from your estate for tax purposes. But at the time you create the trust you may be making gifts that would subject you to gift tax anyway. Further, if the trust is irrevocable, you can no longer be the trustee, control the property, or change who gets what.

In short, you can't change your mind and you part with your assets forever. That's an enormous decision and an expert should be consulted.

Living trusts: the fine print

Living trusts are the subject of much good press lately. They're generally described in glowing—almost too good to be true—terms. And, indeed, there's a lot to commend them. But do not lose sight of the fine print:

Who will be your trustee? Not all states let you be your own trustee. For example, under New York law the person who creates the trust cannot be the trustee if he is the beneficiary as well. In states like New York, you'll have to select a trustee. If you have a spouse, trusted friend, or relative who will serve without a fee, you may want to go ahead.

You must be certain that your trustee has the responsibility and sensitivity to serve in this role. After all, your loved ones will look toward that person when the time arises.

How important is avoiding probate? In some states probate is a lot worse than in others. For example, in Florida there are fewer restraints on the fees that executors can charge. Some people there regard probate as a costly and horrid process to be avoided in all events. In New York, on the other hand, fees of executors are regulated by law, and the process is generally not as costly. For that reason alone, living trusts are enormously popular in Florida where the desire to avoid probate is greater. In New York, avoiding probate is not usually the sole driving force behind setting up a living trust.

Technical tax rules. Many technical rules govern the income taxation of trusts and estates. Assets passing through trusts and estates must be coordinated to pay estate debts, administration expenses, and taxes. In short, at your death, different tax consequences may result depending on how a living trust and its assets coordinate with your probate estate. You will need to consult an expert to determine if a living trust will in fact produce the best tax result in your case.

Bottom line. Your state's rules regarding probate should be reviewed with an expert if that is your primary reason for setting up a living trust. It may be that the cost of setting up the trust and transferring assets is just not worth the trouble or expense in your particular state. Also, whether you can serve as your own trustee may make a difference to you as well.

CHAPTER IV

The federal estate and gift tax

C ongress has given each of us a $600,000 tax exemption on combined lifetime and testamentary gifts. Though the exemption is high, the tax rates are, too. A $3 million taxable estate is in the 55 percent bracket.

If you want to enjoy your property in the here and now and transfer it to your family intact for their subsequent enjoyment, minimizing your tax bite is essential, particularly if you're married and have a combined estate over $600,000.

THE FEDERAL ESTATE TAX

The federal government imposes a tax on the transfer of property upon death. All of the property that you own and pass on at your death is your "gross estate." This is reduced by permitted expenses and deductions, the most significant of which is an unlimited marital deduction that lets you pass everything you own tax-free to a current spouse.

Once your gross estate is reduced by these amounts, a taxable estate is determined. The tax is levied against that amount. However a so-called unified credit of $192,800 is available; it shelters $600,000 of property from tax.

The effective tax rates range from 37 percent to 55 percent of taxable estates. However, as a practical matter, if you're single, the unified credit alone lets you leave a $600,000 estate tax-free. For a married couple, a combined net worth of up to

$1.2 million can avoid estate taxes just by maximizing each spouse's use of the unified credit.

Unified estate and gift taxes

The federal estate tax is part of a unified estate and gift tax system. That means there is a single tax rate schedule that applies to gifts and estates. With some exceptions, everything you own and give away, whether during life or upon death, is added together to figure out your tax liability.

This unification occurs when you are figuring your taxable estate. Add back in all the taxable gifts you've made, plus the tax you've paid. (Taxable gifts are explained in greater detail in Chapter V.) For our purposes here, you should know that you generally can make gifts of up to $10,000 per donee (that is, recipient) per year completely tax-free. These gifts do not figure into your estate taxes.

The unified credit can be used to offset tax on lifetime gifts or your taxable estate. Each individual gets one unified credit and it doesn't matter if it is used during his or her lifetime, or to soak up estate taxes at death.

STATE DEATH TAXES

Keep in mind that these federal rates do not reflect death taxes imposed by some states. A state death tax credit is available in computing federal estate taxes, but it is limited. It does not work the same way as a deduction for state income taxes on your federal income tax return.

State death taxes vary widely from state to state, so they have not been considered in any of the examples provided in this book. However, they may impact on the overall tax picture in states with significant death taxes.

WHAT'S IN YOUR ESTATE FOR TAX PURPOSES?

Everything you own at death, to the extent you own an interest

UNIFIED ESTATE AND GIFT TAX RATES

Precise calculations of estate tax liability are very complicated. This schedule shows current rates, but it should not be used alone to determine actual liability.

Column A Taxable amounts over	Column B Taxable amounts not over	Column C Tax on amount in column A	Column D Rate of tax on excess over amount in column A
$ 0	$ 10,000	$ 0	18%
10,000	20,000	1,800	20%
20,000	40,000	3,800	22%
40,000	60,000	8,200	24%
60,000	80,000	13,000	26%
80,000	100,000	18,200	28%
100,000	150,000	23,800	30%
150,000	250,000	38,800	32%
250,000	500,000	70,800	34%
500,000	750,000	155,800	37%
750,000	1,000,000	248,300	39%
1,000,000	1,250,000	345,800	41%
1,250,000	1,500,000	448,300	43%
1,500,000	2,000,000	555,800	45%
2,000,000	2,500,000	780,800	49%
2,500,000		(see note below)	

NOTE: The rate is scheduled to change in 1992 for taxable amounts over $2,500,000; talk to a good estate tax expert for more advice.

How to use this schedule. Assume you are single and have a taxable estate of $650,000. Look first in column A until you see "Taxable amounts over $500,000" and in column B, "Taxable amounts not over $750,000." In column C, you'll see that the tax on $500,000 is $155,800. In column D you'll see that the excess amount over $500,000 is taxed at a 37 percent rate; $650,000 minus $500,000 is $150,000. A tax of 37 percent on that amount comes to $55,500. Add that amount to $155,800 to get the tentative tax of $211,300. This amount is reduced by the unified credit of $192,800. The estate tax liability is $18,500.

Use the same table to determine gift tax liability. Assume you make a single gift of $200,000. The tax would be computed as follows: First deduct the $10,000 annual exclusion from the $200,000. The tax on the remainder, $190,000, is $38,800 (the tax on $150,000) plus $12,800 (32 percent of $40,000). The total tentative tax is $51,600.

If the unified credit has been fully exhausted, you will owe that amount. Assuming the credit is fully available, you would pay no tax on this gift but would use up $51,600 of your unified credit, leaving a $141,200 credit remaining to offset future gift or estate taxes.

in it, will be included in your estate. Think of the big picture here because the IRS takes an expansive view of what's included. The inclusions are not limited by state law concepts of property subject to probate. For example, even if your nephew is the beneficiary of the $100,000 life insurance proceeds on a policy you owned, that $100,000 is included for federal estate tax purposes.

All of your property is generally valued as of the date you die. Special rules might permit an estate to be valued six months later. Value for this purpose is established in much the same manner as was discussed in Chapter I.

The following types of property are included in your taxable estate:

Property owned by you

This includes your stocks, bonds, furniture, personal effects, jewelry, business interests, artwork, and real estate.

Your share of jointly owned property

Remember this is subject to the rules discussed in Chapter I. If you and someone not your spouse own the property jointly, whether it is real estate or a bank account, it will be fully included in your estate unless the survivor can prove what he or she contributed. Only 50 percent of the value of property jointly owned with a spouse is included.

Other property interests

These include interests you may have as a beneficiary in a trust or the right to determine who will get property.

Paul Ray sets up a trust for his daughter Tina. Tina is to receive the income from the trust for 10 years. At the end of the 10-year period, the trust terminates and the trust principal is to be distributed equally to Tina's children. Tina perishes in a freak tornado during this 10-year period. The value of her remaining income interest will be included in her estate.

Now assume that Paul sets up the trust so that the income

is paid to Tina and, at Tina's death, the principal goes to whomever Tina selects. The value of the trust principal would also be included in Tina's estate. Tina's ability to determine who gets the trust principal is known as a "power of appointment."

Transferred property

Here we are talking about something you give away while still holding something back. Let's look at some real life examples:

Life estates. Phil Levine gives his granddaughter Jane his cabin in the mountains, but retains the right to live in it for life. If Grandpa Phil dies, the cabin would be fully included in his estate. Why? It looks like he parted with his whole interest and at his death didn't "transfer" anything. But this is not so under the tax rules. A property interest that the recipient can only possess or enjoy by surviving you is generally caught in your estate for tax purposes. This makes sense because it's as if Phil only gave away the house when he died.

Survivor annuities. The value of transfers such as joint and survivor annuities, which are measured by your lifespan, are also included in your taxable estate. A joint and survivor annuity, which is a common form of payout from a pension plan, provides a fixed amount of income to a person for life; on that person's death, it continues to a survivor. Even though the first to die never receives the survivor annuity, its value is included in his estate for federal estate tax purposes.

Revocable trusts. If you can take back property that you gave away, it will be included in your estate. For example, if you reserve the right to revoke a trust, the value of the trust remains in your estate. But you do not necessarily have to reserve the right to revoke for this rule to come into play. Lots of tax rules would cause the trust property to be included in your estate if you could control the trustees, change the beneficiaries, or determine what they can receive. Why? Because you would be acting like an owner. If you're too much like the owner, the trust will end up in your taxable estate.

Real life, real answers.

A lice Nelson, a real estate broker, is divorced and has two grown children. Her main assets are a condominium and a vacation house. Under her will, she gave each child the property they preferred and divided whatever cash remained after funeral expenses, etc. At the time of her death, the condo is worth $275,000, the vacation house $250,000, and cash and personal property about $75,000. Her $600,000 estate will pass tax-free to her children because of the unified credit.

It is the value of the assets at death—and not the form of the bequest—that counts for purposes of the unified credit. Alice could have left her property to her children in trust until they each turned 35. The estate tax result is the same as if she had left her property to them outright.

Certain transfers within three years of death

The big issue here is life insurance. If you transfer the ownership of an insurance policy within three years of your death, the entire proceeds of the policy, not just the cost of the policy or cash surrender value, will be included in your estate. To exclude life insurance from your estate, you generally must part with all "incidents of ownership" in the policy.

This three-year rule also applies to other transfers. Let's say you create a revocable trust, but then give up all rights to revoke it. Or you give property away but keep the right to get it back if the beneficiary dies before you (called a reversion). If you give up the right to revoke and/or the right to a reversion within three years of your death, the property that was subject to the right will be in your estate anyway.

USING THE UNIFIED CREDIT

For a single person with an estate of less than $600,000, the unified credit of $192,800 solves the entire federal estate tax

Real life, real answers.

C arl and Barbara Locke have a home, which they own jointly, worth $350,000. Carl owns a $100,000 life insurance policy with Barbara as his beneficiary, a boat worth $100,000, and some stocks, bonds, and cash worth about $50,000. If Carl dies this year and leaves all his property to his wife, his share of the house ($175,000) and all the other assets ($250,000) will pass estate tax–free to Barbara. Because of the unlimited marital deduction, there is no tax liability.

If Barbara dies a few years later, her assets of $600,000 (house at $175,000 plus $425,000 inherited from Carl) can pass estate tax–free to her heirs. However, if the assets appreciate substantially in her hands so that their value at her death exceeds $600,000, the unified credit alone may not do the job of avoiding estate taxes. In that case lifetime gifts to the kids and other strategies can be used to avoid the tax.

problem. You can leave your property to anyone, in any form that you wish, and it will pass free of federal estate tax. It's as simple as that.

The unified credit is your planning foundation even if your estate is larger than $600,000. For a single person with a larger estate, the unified credit can be combined with other tax-reducing strategies discussed in the chapters ahead.

What if you're married?

If you're married, each spouse gets his or her own unified credit. For couples with combined estates under $600,000, it does not matter who dies first or how much they leave to each other or their children. No special action is needed to avoid the federal estate tax. Each person's unified credit alone will do the job. No estate tax will be due on either estate.

For couples with larger estates, the biggest tax planning challenge is avoiding tax in the estate of the second spouse to die. Why? In the estate of the first spouse to die, the unlimited marital deduction and the unified credit go a long way toward avoiding tax. However, in the estate of the surviving spouse, there is no unlimited marital deduction. Planning is required so that the surviving spouse is not left with the hot tax potato.

For couples with a combined estate of under $600,000, there is tremendous flexibility in planning. Assets can pass exactly as you'd like because the unified credit eliminates the tax. Married couples do not have to leave all property to the surviving spouse to avoid losing part of the estate to taxes. If a husband is concerned that his wife won't be generous enough with the kids after he's gone, he can leave some of his assets to his children. He will still avoid federal estate taxes.

If the combined estates of a married couple are worth more than $600,000, and most assets are left to the surviving spouse, the unified credit together with the marital deduction will generally avoid estate taxes on the estate of the first to die. However, if more than $600,000 lands in the hands of the surviving spouse, the unified credit in the second estate won't do the job. Reason: There's no marital deduction in the second estate unless the spouse has remarried.

BYPASS TRUST

In the real life story on page 44, assume instead that Carl Locke leaves a $1 million estate to Barbara. There is no estate tax when Carl dies. When Barbara dies, she leaves the property she inherited from Carl ($1 million) plus her share of the house ($175,000) to her children. The unified credit shelters only $600,000 of assets from federal estate taxes. This results in a $225,000 federal estate tax bill that could easily have been avoided. Carl could have set up what's called a unified credit or bypass trust under his will. The trust is funded with approximately $600,000 of assets that can pass tax-free under the unified credit.

EQUALIZING ESTATES

The second tax avoidance strategy for married couples with combined estates of between $600,000 and $1.2 million is to equalize the estates. If each spouse owns half the value of the total assets, each spouse can be assured of maximizing the unified credit, regardless of who dies first. In the case of our real life couple, Barbara and Carl, Barbara's only asset is her share of the house. If she were to die first, the bulk of her unified credit would be wasted and, at Carl's death, a tax nightmare would result. What happens if the estates are equalized?

Assume a few years have passed and now Carl and Barbara jointly own a home worth $500,000 and a beach house worth $200,000. Their other assets are a $100,000 life insurance policy (owned by Carl), the $100,000 boat (title was transferred to Barbara), $75,000 Carl has socked away in a Keogh plan, and stocks and cash worth $75,000, which are in Barbara's name. Each has an estate worth $525,000. If each sets up a bypass trust under the will, naming the children as beneficiaries, these funds will escape tax in the estate of the second to die.

Careful planning is needed to ensure that the surviving spouse will have enough to live on if the bulk of the assets are left to a unified credit trust for the children. Will the nature of the assets passed to the trust produce a sufficient level of income to support the spouse if the trust will be a primary source of support? Even if less than all the assets sheltered by the unified credit are left in trust, there will be an estate tax savings in the estate of the second spouse.

Leaving all the assets to the surviving spouse, when that spouse will likely have an estate over $600,000, is a sure way to make an unnecessary tax payment to Uncle Sam. This is particularly true if you want the children to end up with everything anyhow.

Real life, real answers.

D an and Beth Gallagher have an estate worth $1 million. The assets are in Dan's name except for Beth's interest in the family home, which is worth $175,000. If a bypass trust is set up under Dan's will, assets will go tax-free out of Dan's estate and bypass Beth's. Here's how:

Carl creates a bypass trust under his will. His will provides that the trust will be funded with the maximum amount that can pass free of estate tax because of the unified credit (that is, $600,000). He leaves the balance of his estate to Beth.

Dan can pretty much write the terms of the trust any way he'd like. For example, the trust could provide that the trustee sprinkle income among Beth and the kids, instead of paying it all to Beth. The trustee can be given the power to use trust principal for Beth to maintain her standard of living. The ultimate objective is for the kids to receive the trust principal on Barbara's death.

By using the trust, $600,000 worth of assets pass to the children, undiminished by federal estate tax. The balance of Dan's estate ($400,000) can pass to Beth protected by the marital deduction.

What happens when Beth dies? The assets in the unified credit trust set up under Dan's will won't be included in her estate. Her estate consists of the $400,000 she inherited from Dan, plus her share of the house ($175,000). Assuming there is no appreciation in assets, her estate will be completely sheltered from tax by the unified credit. Combined estate tax bill on both estates: Zero!

THE MARITAL DEDUCTION

You know the marital deduction is unlimited. If you want to leave everything to your spouse, you're all set. But you may have other plans.

Let's say it's your second marriage and you have children from your first marriage that you'd like to get the bulk of your estate. Your objective won't be to give everything outright to your current spouse. Or suppose you're married to a person who's considerably younger. You're concerned that your estate as well as your spouse will end up in someone else's hands. Or maybe you have a spouse who has no head for managing money. Don't despair. There's more in the marital deduction bag of goodies for you.

But let's back up a minute. You only can take advantage of the marital deduction if you leave property to your spouse. This may sound obvious, but we're talking about someone the IRS considers your spouse: Don't count your former spouse, soon-to-be spouse, or would-be spouse. State laws regarding the validity of a marriage or common law marriage may also have impact here.

Assuming you've passed that hurdle and know whether or not you're married, there are some other marital deduction basics. First, the property must be included in your estate. Second, the interest that passes must generally include all the rights of an owner. That is, your spouse must have the right to possess, enjoy, and dispose of the property. The rights usually cannot terminate. For example, the right to use a house for 10 years is a right that terminates.

Clearly an outright bequest of property to your spouse will qualify for the marital deduction. For example, if you leave 100 shares of Gadget stock outright to your spouse, he or she can possess, enjoy (that is, receive dividends), or sell the stock. You've given over total control. But what happens if you want your surviving spouse to have something less than total control? Can you leave the Gadget stock in trust for your spouse and still qualify for the marital deduction? Yes. There are two main types of trusts that qualify for the marital deduction and yet pass something short of outright control.

The classic marital deduction trust

Under this trust, the surviving spouse is provided with income for life and the power to appoint who will get the trust principal. There's lots of flexibility regarding the powers of the trustee to withdraw principal or even of the surviving spouse to withdraw principal.

The big feature of the classic marital trust is that the management of the fund is taken out of the spouse's hands. A surviving spouse can be protected from the manipulations of children and relatives because control ultimately rests with the trustee. Since the surviving spouse decides who gets the property, you and your spouse should agree on who the ultimate beneficiaries should be before you set up this type of trust. Clearly, it won't work if you're in your second marriage and are afraid that your current spouse may not provide for your children from a prior marriage.

The Q-TIP trust

If you are concerned about providing for children from a prior marriage, or just want to be able to name who ultimately gets the trust principal, the second form of marital deduction trust may be best. It's frequently referred to as a Q-TIP trust, which stands for "qualified terminable interest property trust." In this trust your spouse's rights in the property you leave come to an end when he or she does.

This, of course, runs afoul of the rules regarding the right to possess, enjoy, and dispose, but that's okay. The IRS has created this special case and, if you play by the rules, this type of property transfer will qualify for the marital deduction.

Under the Q-TIP trust, your surviving spouse must be given all of the trust income for life (payable at least annually), but you can determine how the trust principal will be split up when your spouse dies. Essentially, the surviving spouse is given what's called a life estate in the trust assets; the interest terminates on the survivor's death.

One price you pay for taking the marital deduction in the estate of the first spouse to die (that is, the one who sets up the trust) is that the property must also be included in the surviving spouse's estate, even if he or she is not given the right to dispose of the trust property.

With a Q-TIP trust, the powers of the trustee can be as broad or narrow as you desire. There is no requirement that the survivor be given the right to invade the trust or withdraw principal, although these rights are permitted. The only no-no is that the surviving spouse can't have the power to direct trust principal to any other beneficiary during his or her lifetime. This is unlike the classic marital trust where the survivor must be given the right to decide who gets the trust property. With a Q-TIP trust, the survivor can be given the option to do so, but it's not required.

THE CHARITABLE DEDUCTION

Perhaps your wealth is such that being generous is a way of life, or maybe there's no more worthwhile beneficiary than a favorite charity. Whatever the reason, there's an estate tax deduction for gifts to charity. It's another valuable planning tool for singles with estates worth more than $600,000 and married couples with combined estates above $1.2 million. It's a clear case where doing good unto others is good for you, too.

A brief comparison with the personal income tax deduction for charitable contributions may be helpful here. With charitable contributions for income tax purposes, there are some limits. An income tax deduction is limited each year to 50 percent of adjusted gross income, with other limits affecting capital gain property. The good news for estate tax purposes is that you can give it all away and get a full deduction. There's no 50 percent limit. For some, this may be an important planning consideration when weighing the value of a lifetime gift or a gift made under a will.

Outright gifts

An outright gift to a charity will, of course, qualify for the charitable deduction. Remember, we are talking about legitimate IRS-approved charities, entities, or organizations to which contributions are deductible, not just a poor cousin who's down on his luck. With other types of gifts to charities, there are lots of tax rules that spell out what you've got to do to get the deduction.

Charitable bequests in trust

Transfers in trust to charities are permitted and deductible if either the entire interest is transferred or an undivided portion of an interest, such as a remainder interest or life interest, is transferred. Lots of rules come into play here because the IRS wants to be sure it can value your contribution. If you're giving less than your entire interest, such as just the remainder interest (that is, income goes somewhere else first) on certain property, the contribution must be made to a trust.

Charitable remainder trusts

A *charitable remainder annuity trust* is one in which a specific amount can be paid annually to another beneficiary. For example, under this type of trust, you can provide an annuity interest for the life of your spouse or child, with the remainder going to a charity. The amount of the annuity paid to the individual beneficiary must equal at least 5 percent of the value of the property at the time the trust is created (this is determined actuarially).

With a *charitable remainder unitrust*, a fixed percentage of the value of the assets can be paid at least annually to one or more individual beneficiaries. These beneficiaries must be living at the time the trust is created and the value of the interest to them must be at least 5 percent of the trust assets. At the death of the income beneficiary (for up to a 20-year term or a life estate), the underlying property passes to the charity.

Pooled income funds

Another vehicle for making a gift to charity is called a pooled

Real life, real answers.

K atie Ryan made no gifts in her life until she decided to give her son $200,000 to help him purchase a home. This gift was taxable to the extent it exceeded the $10,000 per donee annual gift exclusion. However, when the gift tax return was filed, no gift tax was paid.

Instead the gift ate into roughly $52,000 of the $192,000 "unified credit" available. This credit sheltered the gift from current tax. When Katie dies, the balance of the unified credit can shelter an additional $400,000 (i.e. $600,000 minus $200,000) estate from tax.

If Katie had given her son $600,000 to buy a mansion, she still would have avoided paying current gift tax. But she would have used up her entire unified credit. Thereafter, any assets transferred upon her death would be fully taxable. Also, if Katie continues to make generous lifetime gifts after she uses up her credit, gift tax will have to be paid on gifts that exceed the $10,000 per donee annual exclusion.

income fund. This is an investment fund maintained by the charity to receive bequests.

Under his will, Harry Johnston leaves $100,000 to the Podunk College Pooled Income Fund. These assets are invested along with those contributed by others. Harry's surviving spouse Rita will receive a fixed portion of the fund's earnings for her life. At her death, the $100,000 legacy is Podunk's. On Harry's death, his estate will get a charitable deduction based on the actuarial value of the charity's interest. The value of the deduction will take into account the life income interest paid to Rita.

The primary advantage of a pooled income fund is that it enables you to provide for a surviving beneficiary first, before the assets end up in the charity's hands. A possible downside is that your family loses control over the investment and management of the funds and the individual beneficiary receives only a fixed amount. There's no leeway for emergencies.

Giving to charitable remainder trusts and pooled income funds involves complex rules. Particularly with large estates or where large donations are contemplated, these gifts should be carefully integrated with your overall estate plan to be sure all bases are covered. The input of experts will be required to help you select the type of property that should be the subject of such a gift or bequest and determine tax consequences.

CHAPTER V

The incredible shrinking estate

I f you are single and your estate is above $600,000, there will be a tax bite on the excess. The same is true if you are married with a combined estate above $1.2 million. But if you've got your heart set on not paying one cent in estate taxes, there are strategies that can help toward that end.

For starters, though, it's again time to look earnestly at what you want. It may be that you want to leave everything to your spouse, no matter what the tax bite will be on the death of the survivor. After all, if you have a combined estate of over $1.2 million the children will still end up with plenty. You may not care that some of it will be lost to taxes.

Another possible scenario is that your spouse is currently incapacitated and you'd rather your kids have your estate than have it fall into the hands of a nursing home promising lifetime care. Your focus is not on avoiding the tax bite but rather on seeing your kids get your wealth, should you die first.

Lots of human dramas enter into all the planning possibilities. Avoiding taxes is only one of the factors going in the decision-making process, and it should not necessarily override other considerations. Still, there are several ways you can reduce your taxes and still place your assets in the hands of your desired beneficiaries.

MAKING LIFETIME GIFTS

If you make a gift to someone, that property is gone from your estate. Depending on what the gift is, perhaps more than just that property is out of your estate. Let's say you make a gift of $10,000 worth of stock to a friend. The stock pays dividends and may go up in value. Not only is the stock out of your estate, but so too is the potential appreciation in value, the dividends, and even the earnings on those dividends over time.

Under the tax law, there is a $10,000 per donee annual gift tax exclusion. The only big catch is that the gift must be of a present interest. If Burt says today, "Ellie, you can have my house when I'm gone," Ellie doesn't have a present interest. She won't have the gift until a future date. For the gift to qualify for the $10,000 exclusion, the recipient generally has to have the right to use the gift presently.

If a gift is made of income from a trust, that may qualify for the annual exclusion even though the recipient doesn't ever get the trust principal. For certain gifts to minors, the $10,000 exclusion is available even though the child can't use the money until he or she is older. But again, certain conditions must be met.

What it boils down to is you can make gifts of up to $10,000 to as many people as you want each year without incurring gift tax. With a planned giving program, it is possible to greatly cut down the size of your estate.

PLANNED GIVING PROGRAMS

Bob and Clara Burwell have five grandchildren. If Bob wants to give each grandchild $10,000 this year, he will reduce his estate by $50,000 and won't pay a penny in tax. Bob's other option is to give gifts to his spouse; this can be done in any amount, tax-free. But that won't solve the problem of reducing their combined estates.

In fact, if Bob and Clara agree to make "split gifts," where the

Real life, real answers.

M arvin and Emma Tashian have a combined estate of over $2 million. They have done what they can to equalize their estates and each has $1 million in assets. Each of their wills provides for a maximum bypass trust ($600,000) with their two children as the beneficiaries. Any amount above $600,000 will pass to the surviving spouse.

When Emma dies, Marvin inherits $400,000 and he becomes the owner of a $1.4 million estate ($1 million of his own money, plus the $400,000 he inherits from Emma).

Of this $1.4 million, only $600,000 will be sheltered from federal estate tax by his unified credit. If he takes no action (assuming the property doesn't appreciate in his hands), he's looking at an estate tax bill of $320,000.

But, if Marvin begins a program of annual gifts to his two children and five grandchildren, he could reduce his estate by $70,000 annually. In a period of five years, his potential estate could be reduced by $350,000. This would essentially cut his estate tax bill in half: from $320,000 to about $153,000. More than the amount of the tax bite is gone from his estate, but part of it is in his kids' hands, not Uncle Sam's.

gift is treated as being half made by each of them regardless of who originally owned the underlying property, they can give $20,000 to each grandchild. They would reduce their combined estates by $100,000 and still not incur any gift tax at present, or estate tax on the assets transferred out. By limiting their gifts to the annual exclusion, the unified credit remains intact to shelter their estates.

For people with substantial estates, whether single or married, a planned program of gift giving can accomplish several ends. It can provide for your beneficiaries, perhaps at a time when they can really use the funds. It can reduce the size of your estate without any present tax cost to you and, ultimately, your estate tax bill goes down. It gets the property in the hands of those you'd like to have it. Money that would have gone to Uncle Sam is paid to your beneficiaries instead.

There's no doubt that a program of planned gifts is effective at reducing an estate tax bill. But, there are reasons it may not work for everyone. First, you've got to be comfortable and secure enough to give away substantial sums of money. Second, the specter of health problems and unforeseen emergencies is a valid reason for pause. Third, there's the politics of giving away your money while you're alive.

You may want to help a child buy a home, start a business, or cover his other expenses. In that case, present reasons for making the gifts will have the added benefit of reducing your estate. Then again you may have no desire to give away control of your assets while you're alive. That's not uncommon either. All of these factors should be taken into account, making this an entirely personal decision.

HOW TO MAKE GIFTS

The mechanics of making a gift are not always clear. Certainly, a direct transfer of physical property itself, be it cash, stock, or a painting, will accomplish the goal. But gifts can take other forms as well. For example, a gift is made if you forgive a debt that someone owes you. If Bill lends his son $20,000 for a down payment on a house, and then later says his son doesn't have to pay him back, he's made a gift of $20,000. In this context, other issues may arise as well, particularly whether a loan was intended in the first place. Depending on how the transaction is cast, different income tax treatment may result.

GIFTS IN TRUST

Gifts can also be made in trust. As discussed in Chapter III, a variety of provisions can be included in a trust to have it accomplish whatever goals you set out. In order to make a full-fledged gift in trust, there are certain things you must clearly part with, for both income and estate tax purposes. You cannot reserve the right to revoke or terminate the trust; change beneficiaries or vary the amounts each may receive; hasten or increase any beneficiary's enjoyment of the property; or get at the principal of the trust.

As a general matter, if you reserve these rights as a trustee, the property may still be included in your estate. For example, assume Sam creates a trust with his three children as beneficiaries. He does not reserve the right to alter, amend, or revoke the trust. Sam names himself as trustee. Under the trust agreement, the trustee has the power to sprinkle income among the three children. Since Sam can determine the amounts each beneficiary can receive, he will be treated as the owner of the trust property and it will be included in his taxable estate when he dies.

Access to trust funds—Crummey powers

If property is transferred in trust, there are two rights or powers that a beneficiary may be given that have important tax consequences. The first is a "Crummey" power, so named after the case that involved the issue. Under a Crummey power, if the beneficiary is given the right to demand trust property, then gifts to the trust will be eligible for the $10,000 annual gift tax exclusion. This can be important where a trust does not pay out income or principal currently, but where funds are accumulated. If the beneficiary does not have access to the funds for a reasonable period of time, a gift to the trust does not qualify as a present interest for purposes of the annual exclusion.

A Crummey power is frequently featured in life insurance trusts. Such trusts generally have a life insurance policy as their only asset. The trust's value is usually very small until the insured dies. Then the trust is funded with the death proceeds from the insurance policy.

If the terms of the trust give the trust beneficiaries a Crummey power, funds put in the trust to pay the premiums and maintain the insurance will not be subject to gift tax to the extent they're under the $10,000 annual exclusion amount.

Five and five power

The second form of power that has tax ramifications is called a five and five power. It generally refers to the right of an income beneficiary to withdraw the greater of 5 percent or $5,000 of trust principal each year. Why is it important?

Let's look at Jennifer and Max Downey. They're married with a combined gross estate of around $1.2 million. They have equalized their estates and each has set up a bypass trust under his/her will. The bypass trusts, which do not qualify for the marital deduction, provide that income can be sprinkled among the surviving spouse and children. However, there is concern on the part of both spouses that they may not have enough to live on.

That concern is not far-fetched because of the nature of the assets in their estates. The main asset is a home ($750,000) in joint names, an interest in a closely held business ($300,000) in Max's name, and investments ($400,000) mainly in Jennifer's name. If Jennifer dies first, Max will own the house and the business, but most of the investments will be used to fund the trust. What if Max's business turns sour and he can't sell it? Or what if Max becomes ill and the business becomes worthless without him? Would Jennifer have wanted Max to have to sell the house to live? Probably not.

If the unified credit trust under Jennifer's will is funded with liquid assets and Max is given a five and five power, he has a right to withdraw annually up to 5 percent of the value of the trust or $5,000, whichever is greater. Depending on the survivor's lifestyle, the liquidity and earning power of the assets he inherits, and an element of luck, there are legitimate concerns regarding what will be enough. There's no reason to end up poor in the name of tax planning. A five and five power can take the sting out. Even better, Max's access to trust principal won't cause the entire trust to be included in his estate.

TRANSFERS OF JOINTLY OWNED PROPERTY

Spouses can make unlimited gifts to each other and transfers of jointly held property are no exception. If you take title to a home in your name and later decide to transfer it into joint ownership with your spouse, no gift tax consequences result. If either of you dies, only half the value of the house will be included in the deceased spouse's estate, regardless of who paid what. Or you can transfer the home entirely into your spouse's name. Nothing will be included in your estate when you die.

This is not the case with transfers of jointly held property with anyone other than a spouse. If a joint tenancy is created between unmarried people, a taxable gift is made to the extent someone receives more than he or she paid for.

John Golde wants to help his daughter Stephanie open a bookstore. He purchases a $100,000 building downtown for the business. John and Stephanie take title as joint tenants even though he paid for the building. A gift of half the value of the building is made to Stephanie at the time the building is purchased. A gift tax return must be filed, but any tax accruing may be shielded by John's unified credit. When John dies, the building will be fully included in his estate, since he paid for it. Stephanie will own it outright on her dad's death.

Now assume that Stephanie put up $25,000 of the $100,000 purchase price. When her father dies, the building is worth $200,000. What happens now? The appreciation attributable to John's $75,000 contribution will also go into his estate. Here John's interest in the building will be $150,000 for estate tax purposes.

THE BASIS OF THE GIFT

Once you decide to make a gift, it's important to consider the basis of the property that you will give. "Basis" is generally what you paid for the property, or what it cost you. If you buy a painting for $25,000, you have a $25,000 basis in the painting. Your basis is the starting point for measuring gain or loss when you subsequently sell the property.

When you make a gift, the recipient's basis is the basis the property had in your hands, a "carryover basis." There can be an upward adjustment if the donor pays a gift tax.

If Jim Fiardi buys a cottage for $75,000 and gives it to his daughter Roseann, her basis is $75,000. If she turns around and sells the property for $125,000, she'll pay income tax on $50,000 worth of gain. If she's in the 28 percent tax bracket, she'll lose $14,000 to taxes.

Compare this with the situation with inherited property. Let's say Jim never made a gift of the property to Roseann and instead left it to her under his will. When he dies, the cottage is worth $125,000. If Roseann turns around and sells the cottage for $125,000, how will she fare? She'll pocket the full amount. There will be no taxable gain on the sale because her basis in the property is the fair market value on Jim's death.

With inherited property you get a "step-up" in basis. The basis is stepped-up to the property's value on the owner's death and you're not stuck with the owner's basis, which is presumably lower.

The distinction in the basis for property acquired by gift as compared with devise (by will) presents many planning opportunities. Let's say that Jim has decided to give Roseann some funds to help her buy a cottage of her own. He decides to take advantage of the $10,000 annual exclusion so he's going to begin making gifts of stock to her. He's got two blocks of stock, each worth $10,000. The ABC stock has a $2,000 basis and the XYZ stock has a $9,000 basis. If Roseann is going to convert the stock to cash, she'll lose a big chunk of it to taxes if Jim transfers the low-basis ABC stock.

As a general rule, if you have greatly appreciated property, you're better off holding on to it and passing it on at your death. The donee gets a better deal if you make a gift of the high basis property. This is best illustrated in the case of a home. Many people own homes they bought years ago. It's not uncommon to have a $30,000 basis in a $500,000 home. If you're thinking of giving property, you may be better off holding on to your home. Then your heirs can take advantage of the step-up in basis at your death. In either case, it depends, of course, on how old you are and whether you want to hold on to the property.

It should be noted that with property acquired under the right of survivorship in a joint tenancy, even the survivor gets a step-up for the share held by the deceased tenant. Bruce and Luanne O'Reilly are married and their $500,000 home is in joint names. They paid $100,000 for the home 10 years ago. When Bruce dies, half the value of the home ($250,000) is included in his estate. Luanne now owns the home outright and her basis in it is $300,000. How? Her original share of the basis was $50,000 and she gets the step-up in basis equal to the date of death value ($250,000) on the share she inherits from Bruce.

UNIFORM GIFTS TO MINORS ACT

One popular way to make a gift to a minor is under the Uniform Gifts to Minors Act (UGMA), which has been adopted by most states. Under UGMA, the gift is made to a custodian who holds and manages the property, usually cash, stocks, or bonds, until the child reaches the age of majority. The property is turned over to the child at age 21, or earlier if the state's law deems the child to have legal capacity earlier, perhaps at age 18. The gift is registered in the name of the custodian, even though for gift tax purposes the gift is made to the child.

Gifts under UGMA are "present interests" and therefore eligible for the $10,000 gift tax exclusion. This is very important because it enables you to make gifts to young children, put them in "trust" at relatively low cost, and accumulate earnings during the period of their minority.

There are a couple of catches. To the extent that UGMA funds are spent on items that come under the umbrella of legal support, which a parent is supposed to provide, they will be taxed to the parent if he is the custodian. The definition of a support obligation is a matter of state law. For example, whether a parent is obligated to pay for private school is determined locally.

The other catch concerns how the funds in the custodial account are taxed. If they are not spent on support obligations and are either accumulated during the period or spent on other things, the income will be taxed to the child. Under the 1986 tax law's "kiddie tax," investment income of children under the age of 14 is taxed at the parents' highest rate, except for the first $1,000, which will be taxed in the child's tax bracket. Consider investments that defer income until the child is 14.

Shifting income

Under present law, with essentially a two-bracket system, there are only limited income-shifting possibilities. But there can be significant tax savings for UGMA funds for children over age 14 who are in the 15 percent bracket.

Mark Wefer has made gifts under UGMA to his son Charley, now 15. The UGMA gifts are now worth $100,000 and earn roughly 10 percent or $10,000 a year. If the earnings are simply reinvested, they will be taxed in Charley's 15 percent bracket and $1,500 will be lost to taxes. If Mark is in the 33 percent bracket and either hasn't put the funds in a UGMA custodial account or uses the funds for support, he will pay $3,300 in taxes on the same $10,000 earnings. Here it's clear that tax savings within the family unit are doubled by the creation of the UGMA account. Also, the earnings on the tax savings create an even greater pot at the end of the rainbow.

Custodianship

The big caveat with custodianship is that if you make a gift to your child and are the custodian as well, the property will be included in your estate if you die while the child is still a minor. This can be avoided if you are not the custodian with respect to gifts you make.

The Uniform Gifts to Minors Act is an easy way to give a custodian the authority to deal with property for a minor. Since minors cannot legally invest or deal with certain assets, much red tape is involved if assets are put directly in a minor's name. UGMA custodial accounts are a preferable alternative to the costly and cumbersome prospect of appointing a guardian to manage property for a minor.

The appointment of a guardian generally requires court approval and guardians are frequently subject to bonding and accounting requirements as well. Some states require court approval for every expenditure, down to the last piano lesson or doctor's bill. Gifts under UGMA avoid this red tape.

THE 2503(c) TRUST

There are two types of trusts that are particularly helpful for making gifts to children. Let's say you'd like to set up a gift-giving program of $10,000 to each of your three children each year, but you do not want them to be able to draw upon the money. Ordinarily, this type of gift wouldn't qualify for the exclusion because it's not considered a present interest if the recipient cannot spend the money. The way around this is a 2503(c) trust, so named for the section of the tax law that authorizes it.

If you follow the rules, these gifts in trust will be eligible for the annual exclusion. The trust must provide that the trust property and income may be spent only by or for the benefit of the child until he or she is 21. At that point any assets remaining in the trust generally are turned over to the child. If the child dies before age 21, the trust funds must be paid to his or her estate or as the child designates, if applicable.

In some ways a 2503(c) trust is similar to a custodial account under UGMA. But here there is no risk that the funds will wind up in your estate. Also, if state law would give the child UGMA funds at age 18, it may be preferable to have the extra three years, until age 21.

THE CRUMMEY TRUST

The second way to make a gift in trust for a child and still take advantage of the annual exclusion is by using a Crummey right. A Crummey right is the power of a beneficiary to demand trust principal. In the context of a trust for a minor, this means that the child must be given the right to demand the property. This may appear to be a drawback, but in reality it may not be an issue with young children or older children who understand your goals, tax and otherwise. There is clearly a risk if your child does not understand that the funds *should not be withdrawn*.

The advantage of using this form of trust is that the trust is not required to terminate when the child turns 21. For many parents, turning over substantial funds to a 21 year old may provide little comfort. They would rather keep the funds in trust until the child is older.

SPECIAL CONSIDERATIONS

Apart from the special rules for making gifts to children, there are special rules for certain types of expenses that may be particularly important for younger people. Payments of tuition directly to an educational institution, and payments for medical care directly to a provider, are not considered transfers subject to gift tax. Accordingly, they will not eat into the $10,000 annual gift tax exclusion.

For educational expenses to be gift tax–free, payments must be for tuition only. Expenses for room, board, books, etc. won't qualify. Great planning opportunities exist here, particularly if generous grandparents are in the picture.

Speaking of grandparents, a word of caution is due. There

is a "generation-skipping" transfer tax that is designed to tax transfers that skip a generation, that is from grandparent to grandchild. It is intended to catch those gifts in trust that are made by parents to their children, and then their children's children. Each person has a $1 million specific exemption so the generation-skipping tax clearly affects only the wealthy. However, it is extremely complex and should be reviewed with a tax adviser if you're even in the ballpark.

TRANSFERRING LIFE INSURANCE

Life insurance can help you accomplish many estate planning goals. Life insurance proceeds can enlarge a modest estate, provide for your family while your assets are tied up in administration, and even provide funds for the estate tax bill in large estates with no liquid assets.

Life insurance has unique advantages in the context of estate planning. During your life, a policy's cash value builds up year after year, sheltered from income tax. On your death, the life insurance proceeds are excluded from the taxable income (that is, are not subject to income tax) of your beneficiary. Because life insurance is an asset that may have a relatively small value while you are alive, and far greater worth after your death, it presents many planning opportunities.

One major planning consideration is whether the insured should remain the owner of a policy on his or her life. If the owner gives up control over the policy (that is, gives up the right to change the beneficiary, etc.), there is a unique tax advantage. Not only will the policy be out of his or her estate for estate tax purposes, but the proceeds will also be income tax–free to the beneficiary.

Consider Roger's situation. He and his only child Mike own and operate a shopping center. Roger owns the property, which is worth $2 million. The balance of Roger's assets consists of investments worth about $500,000. Roger is a widower and on his death he leaves everything to his son. The $2.5 million estate has an estate tax bill of $823,000. But with only $500,000 in liquid assets, the estate is short over $300,000 in cash to cover the tax bill. The executor is left with a couple of alternatives: sell or refinance. Had insurance been taken in Roger's name, the result would have been different.

What would have happened if Roger had taken out a $750,000 life insurance policy, with his estate as the beneficiary? The size of his estate would have been increased ($3.25 million) and his tax bill would have been $1,225,500. But the insurance together with his investments would have covered the federal estate tax bill.

Life insurance as an asset also adds flexibility to an estate plan. Assume that, as time goes on, Roger's shopping center declines in value to $1 million because the area has deteriorated. Roger's investment assets retain their value ($500,000) and will clearly be sufficient to cover the tax bill ($363,000). But Roger has already purchased the $750,000 policy.

If he dies while owning the policy, what happens? His estate will be jacked up from $1.5 to $2.25 million. So, too, with the tax bill: from $363,000 to $710,500. Most of the insurance proceeds will be given to the IRS, a result that can be avoided. How? Roger can transfer the policy to Mike, and get the proceeds out of his taxable estate.

A couple of important rules come into play here. Transferring a policy is no small matter. You've really got to give up everything, no strings attached. You cannot keep the right to change beneficiaries, surrender, cancel, or assign the policy, pledge the policy for a loan, or obtain its cash surrender value. For Roger, with one son who is his business partner, the decision may be easy. For many others, it is a tougher choice.

There's one more rule. After you've given up all these privileges of ownership, *do not die for three years!* That's one of the hardest rules to guarantee in estate planning. If you die within three years after the transfer or gift of an insurance policy, the value of the proceeds will be included in your estate anyhow. For that reason, transferring a policy is not a good deathbed strategy.

There is another part to this three-year rule. Let's say Roger transferred the policy five years before he died, but continued to pay the premiums within the three years before he died. The policy may still be included in his estate.

Irrevocable insurance trusts

Irrevocable insurance trusts are frequently the repository for transferred life insurance policies. They're a very popular tool today. They can be created during your lifetime or under your will. If the insured dies more than three years after the transfer, the proceeds will be out of the insured's estate.

Let's assume Roger has remarried and would like to provide for his new wife as well as his son. He can do just that with an irrevocable insurance trust:

Roger Mellow
Irrevocable Life Insurance Trust

I, Roger Mellow, hereby create the Roger Mellow Irrevocable Life Insurance Trust. I appoint my brother Joe Mellow as trustee. I am irrevocably transferring to the trustee all my right, title, and interest in the life insurance policies listed on the attached schedule. I want my trustee to hold and use the policies in accordance with the following instructions:

1. The trustee shall have all the ownership rights, powers, interest, and benefits of any kind relating to the insurance policies. I retain no such interest or right.

2. The trustee shall invest or reinvest the trust assets as appropriate. He shall use trust income to pay the premiums on the insurance policies.

3. At my death, the trustee shall collect the insurance proceeds and distribute the trust assets as follows:

a. If my wife Mary Mellow shall survive me, the trustee shall give her $50,000 outright to help her manage during the initial period after my death. Thereafter she shall receive all of the income from the trust, payable quarterly, for the rest of her life.

b. If my wife shall not survive me, or upon her death, the trustee shall distribute the remaining trust assets to my son Mike.

4. My trustee shall have all powers conferred by state law.

5. My trustee shall receive compensation for his services in accordance with the statutory schedule.

6. If my trustee cannot act as trustee for any reason, I appoint my sister Lisa Mellow as successor trustee.

7. This agreement cannot be amended, altered, or revoked by me.

_____

Roger Mellow

_____

Joe Mellow, as "Trustee"

Funds in an insurance trust can be used, allocated, or distributed in any way that other trust funds are directed. The trust might also include a provision enabling it to receive assets from other sources. For example, if the trustee is authorized to receive additional property from other sources, this trust may be named as the beneficiary of qualified plan benefits payable to Roger. Again, the terms of the trust can be as flexible as you'd like, once you part with ownership of the insurance policy.

If you create an insurance trust that you can revoke, there will be no tax advantage. However, as discussed in Chapter VII, the proceeds will avoid probate, which may be more important in your case. A transfer of the policy or funds to pay premiums would be a transfer subject to gift tax. It may be eligible for the annual exclusion if a Crummey power is given to the trust beneficiaries.

CHAPTER VI

Transferring assets: other strategies

The incredible shrinking estate is a very big topic. There are lots of ways to reduce your estate and the preceding chapter outlined the main techniques used by the vast majority of people. But there are other strategies that have much to commend them, even if they're not necessarily for everyone. They address more specialized situations.

TRANSFERRING YOUR BUSINESS

Owning your own business can be an income tax delight, with the dual blessing of controlling the books and the players. While it no doubt has its headaches, the family business also may be the centerpiece of your estate plan. It probably has been the sustainer of your family and maybe even the employer of more than just one of you. It's a combination of assets, enormous effort, good will, and lots of family politics, particularly when some family members work in the business and others do not.

Many factors come into play here. First, there's the matter of the business's value. That alone could fill a book. Suffice it to say, expert input is needed here, whether or not you plan to sell it or bequeath it. If you do not work out a value, you might get stuck with the IRS estimate. If enough is at stake, the odds are the government will challenge your valuation in any case. So start marshaling your own arguments on this issue.

Next come your plans for the business. Following are the common scenarios:

- [ ] Plans are in place for partners to buy you out.
- [ ] You want to leave your business in the hands of family members who work in it now.
- [ ] The business derives solely from your personal efforts and will be worth little when you're gone.
- [ ] You can't deal with your own mortality and have put off thinking about this.

Let's look at some of these more closely. If plans are in place for partners to buy you out, you're already familiar with expert input. Somebody, probably a lawyer, has worked out a buy-sell agreement, so that surviving owners or the business itself maintains insurance to buy out a deceased owner's interest from surviving family members. Here's how it works:

Ned, Ted, and Fred own a plumbing contracting business. Ned owns 50 percent, Ted owns 30 percent, and Fred owns 20 percent. They are working owners and the earnings are sufficient to provide for their respective families. However, if one of them is out of the picture, they are concerned about how to protect their business while providing for their families.

First, they establish a value for the business. Sometimes industry guidelines regarding particular types of businesses can be obtained from trade associations and the like. That may be a starting point. The values may be expressed as a multiple of annual earnings or commissions or billings. Let's say the three men determine that their business is worth $300,000. Since the business is labor-intensive and not cash-rich, insurance may be the best way to come up with buyout money.

Either the business can purchase the insurance to effectively redeem the deceased owner's interest, or the fellow owners can purchase the insurance. For example, Ned and Ted would purchase insurance on Fred ($60,000), Ted and Fred would purchase insurance on Ned ($150,000), and Fred and

Ned would purchase insurance on Ted ($90,000). When an owner dies, the surviving owners can use the death proceeds to buy out the interest from the estate of the decedent.

Insurance premiums paid by the owners are not deductible for income tax purposes, but the death proceeds are income tax–free. Also, the amount paid to the survivors will increase the surviving owners' respective bases in their interests in the business.

If the business buys the insurance, premiums are not deductible, but the proceeds are generally income tax–free. However, if the business is in corporate form, as opposed to a partnership, the proceeds may be subject to the corporate alternative minimum tax. In addition, the surviving owners may not receive a step-up in basis if they sell their stock because the corporation paid for the premium.

A buyout arrangement should be nailed down in a properly drawn agreement. It will have the effect of substantiating the value of the business for estate tax purposes, locking in the agreement of the parties, and providing the funding for the deal.

While insurance-funded buyouts are a popular vehicle, they do not necessarily fit in all cases. Maybe it is your intention to make gifts of the business to family members at the helm. But suppose the business is your chief asset and you'd also like to provide for family members who don't work in the business. The situation gets stickier.

Let's look at Dick and Marge Green and their two kids Victor and Cindy. Dick owns a real estate agency. His son Victor is in his mid-thirties and has been working with his dad for several years. Neither Marge nor Cindy work in the agency. Dick would like to pass the business to his son, who he thinks is capable and hardworking. But Dick also wants to be sure his wife is taken care of and his children benefit equally. It's a pretty tall order considering the business can't afford to keep Marge and Cindy on a dole when Dick's no longer working. The money won't be there.

There are a couple of basic solutions here. Dick can sell the business to Victor, buy insurance for Marge and Cindy, or save hefty sums for retirement and use those funds for Marge and Cindy. Another idea is to sign an employment contract with the business that obligates the business to pay the widow an annuity.

If Dick owns the entire business at his death, it will be included in his estate for tax purposes. If he leaves it to his son, the estate may be subject to tax if the unified credit is insufficient to cover it and the balance of the assets avoid tax because of the marital deduction.

If a sale to his son is in order, the same issues regarding the value of the business will arise. Care will have to be taken regarding the structure of the deal, whether it's a sale, gift, or a bit of both. Plus, tough new tax rules affect transfers of appreciated property to family members. The advice of an expert will be needed here.

These tough rules particularly affect businesses that operate in corporate form. Common arrangements in the past included creating two classes of stock, one voting, the other nonvoting. The parent might then give nonvoting stock to a nonworking spouse or child, who could then participate in the profits but not the operation of the business. A big problem here may be resentment on the part of the working family members who have to produce dividends for nonproducers. In a family context, this may be tricky.

But today's tax rules may cause the underlying asset (the business itself) to be brought back into your estate if the restructuring or recapitalization of the business doesn't follow the tough new tax rules. If family members own a substantial interest in the business (for example, 10 percent or more of the voting power or income stream or both), and one member transfers a disproportionately large share while keeping income or rights in it, an *estate tax disaster* will result. So too if the money family members use to buy you out comes from you. At this writing, the IRS has just issued new rules in this area, and legislation is pending that would repeal the whole scheme. You'll need to consult an expert to see where you stand.

Transferring a closely held business is often the most complex and challenging aspect of estate planning. It cuts across a complicated landscape of family, business, and tax turf. The transactions themselves and the family politics that accompany them demand the input of experts.

GRANTOR-RETAINED INCOME TRUSTS (GRITs)

Estate "freezing" refers to planning techniques aimed at keeping a constant value for your estate, that is, getting rid of assets that will appreciate. It's particularly an issue for couples worth upward of $1.2 million or singles worth above $600,000. And with each year's tax legislation, freezing is getting harder to do.

In the wake of the latest changes, so-called grantor-retained income trusts (GRITs) have become popular. Who's the grantor? You are, if you're the person who transfers assets into a trust. And, if you keep the right to receive income or use the property, you have "retained income." Put it all together and you've put assets in trust and kept the income. But there's more.

A GRIT is an *irrevocable* trust set up for a fixed period of years or until the grantor's death, if sooner. The person who creates it can keep the right to income; when the term ends, what's left goes to beneficiaries. Let's consider Eddie DeLuca, who is 68 years old and has recently been acknowledging that he's not getting any younger. He wants to give his daughter Lisa some property, but is not quite ready to cut himself out of the picture.

Eddie recently acquired income-producing property that he thinks should greatly appreciate in value. If he transfers the property to a GRIT for his daughter, he can have his cake and eat it, too. Under the trust agreement, he keeps the income for 10 years. At the end of the 10 years, or if he dies sooner, the property will pass outright to Lisa.

What does the GRIT do for Eddie? Let's look at all the pieces. First, when the trust is set up, gifts are made. Since Lisa gets the property in 10 years, not today, the gifts will not qualify for the $10,000 annual gift tax exclusion. A gift tax return will be required, although any actual tax liability may be shielded by Eddie's unified credit.

What is the value of the gift? It's what the property is worth at the end of 10 years. That is determined actuarially on the date of the transfer. If Eddie outlives the 10 years, the property will be out of his estate. The goal is to get the property and its appreciation out of his estate, so he should expect to outlive the term of the trust. If Eddie has been told he has two years to live, he should either shorten the period or try another strategy. If he doesn't outlive the trust term, the property will be included in his estate.

The timing of the trust term is what's important here. The rules say Eddie can't be the trustee; he can only receive the income the property actually produces (not a fixed annuity); and he can't retain his interest for more than 10 years.

There are two big trade-offs in using a GRIT. First, you are making a gift of the "remainder"—what is left of the property after the income interest terminates. The gift won't qualify for the annual exclusion because it is not a present interest, that is, the beneficiary can't "enjoy" the property until the conclusion of the "retained income" interest. Therefore, you may owe a gift tax if it is not shielded by your unified credit. In that case, you will be eating into your unified credit.

Second, your beneficiaries get your basis in the property transferred to trust; they lose out on the step-up that comes with your death. Careful planning is needed to see if getting the appreciation out and reducing your estate tax outweighs incurring a present gift tax. The value of the gift will be critical in reaching this decision. Since you are making a gift of the remainder, the value is determined actuarially, based on your age and the value of the underlying property.

To see what this means, let's look at Eddie DeLuca again.

The basis for the property he transferred to the GRIT is $200,000. That will be Lisa's basis in the property when it's paid out from the trust. If the property is sold at the end of the trust term for $500,000, Lisa will have a taxable $300,000 gain.

How would the ultimate beneficiary fare if the property was never put in trust? Let's say Lisa inherited the property when it was worth $500,000. They'd each get a $500,000 stepped-up basis. If she turned around and sold the property, there would be no gain.

The other side of the coin, though, is that if Eddie lives out the trust term he will get $500,000 worth of property out of his estate. This must be weighed against the cost of making the gift today.

It's important to carefully consider the property you put into a GRIT. The goal is to give an asset that will appreciate significantly, so the appreciation will be out of your estate. If you think a GRIT may be for you, consult an expert. You will need his or her input regarding valuing the asset, determining the life interest, and the amount of the gift.

The GRIT is one way to get a valuable asset and its appreciation out of your estate. The theory is that if you transfer the property to your beneficiaries earlier rather than later, you'll get all the appreciation out of your estate. But as you'll see, a GRIT isn't the only way to do it.

SALE OF A REMAINDER INTEREST

With a GRIT, you're making a gift of the remainder in trust. The value of the gift is based on the value of what's left when the trust term expires. The same concept applies to the sale of a remainder. Assume Eddie keeps possession of the property for his life, but *sells* the remainder to his daughter Lisa. By structuring the transaction as a sale, it is possible nothing will be included in Eddie's estate.

To determine the value of the remainder, actuarial tables are needed. For a 68 year old, Eddie's retained "life estate" is worth 64 percent of the property's value; the remainder is worth 36 percent. (If Eddie were only 50 years old, the remainder would be worth only 15 percent of the property's total value.) Since the property is valued at $100,000, Lisa can purchase the remainder for $36,000. By selling the remainder now, the property is out of Eddie's estate, no matter how much the property is worth at his death.

Two pointers here. First, if Eddie wants to make a gift of the remainder it *won't* qualify for the annual $10,000 exclusion. A remainder is not a *present* interest, since Lisa can't enjoy the benefits of ownership now. Also, introducing a gift element may open the whole transaction up to challenge. The IRS could argue that the property should be included in Eddie's estate (at its higher date of death value) because there really wasn't a genuine sale to Lisa.

PRIVATE ANNUITIES

Let's say one of Eddie's major concerns is that he's not sure he's going to have enough income to support himself as he gets older. This, coupled with his desire to give his daughter the property, may make a private annuity a good choice. A private annuity is a lot like an annuity sold by an insurance company in that you transfer a chunk of money and receive an annuity (a regular income) in return. In Eddie's situation, he would transfer the property to Lisa and she would agree to pay him an annuity for life.

How does it work? The value of the annuity that Lisa pays her dad must equal the value of the property. If the annuity is worth less than the property, a gift has been made (to Lisa). But if a gift is made, it is a present interest since the property is Lisa's right away, and it can be shielded by the $10,000 annual gift tax exclusion.

The private annuity is essentially a sale, with payments made over the life of the seller. Eddie will report the gain on the sale over time as he receives annuity payments. Part of each payment will be a tax-free return of capital (up to Eddie's basis) and part will be gain if it's worth more than he paid when he sells it to Lisa. Lisa will get no tax deduction for the payments to Eddie.

However, if it is income-producing property, she'll have the property's earnings (and depreciation deductions) to help her make the annuity payments. As an estate-planning matter, the property and appreciation are out of Eddie's estate and he's got a stream of income for life.

Special tax rules govern all intrafamily sales. Again, you will need to consult an adviser about how long the annuity term should be, the value of the property, and the best property to transfer under this arrangement.

INSTALLMENT SALES

An installment sale is very much like a private annuity, except the sales price is not structured as an annuity. It's just a payout over a period of time, like a mortgage or any other loan for that matter. Installment sales can be made to anyone, but special rules apply to family sales. Normally, with an installment sale, part of each payment is return of capital, part is gain, and part is interest on the unpaid amount. However, if you sell to a related party (a child, grandchild, or spouse) and that family member resells, that resale will trigger immediate recognition of all the gain. Problems will arise if you forgive installments as they come due.

CHAPTER VII

Probing probate

Probate is the process of carrying out the wishes expressed in your will with court supervision. The process involves having your will accepted as valid, valuing your assets, paying off creditors, paying taxes, and distributing the balance of the assets to heirs or to beneficiaries.

Probate affects only those assets that you solely own at your death, or that you own as a tenant in common. Other property, including jointly owned property with a right of survivorship, life insurance, and proceeds received under qualified plans, will automatically pass to designated survivors. Such assets are not caught up in the court-supervised probate process. However, estate administration will include settling those assets.

Probate has become a negative term, connoting too much red tape and unnecessary expense. We've all been told to avoid it. This chapter will enlighten you as to some of the particulars.

WHAT HAPPENS TO AN ESTATE AT DEATH?

Dear old Harry Lynch is gone. He left behind Joan, his wife, three grown children, and an $800,000 estate. The house he owned jointly as tenants by the entirety with his wife, worth $400,000, is all hers. She also got the proceeds from a $100,000 life insurance policy and $300,000 worth of retirement benefits from Harry's IRAs and pension plans. Under his will, Harry left each of his children $100,000 worth of stock. Some smaller bank accounts ($15,000) and a brand-new car ($30,000) also went to Joan. His brother-in-law Larry has been named as executor. Where do we go from here?

At the moment Harry died, he passed along his property to others. Collecting his assets, preserving them, investing and safekeeping them, are all aspects of settling the estate. So too are paying the estate's debts, taxes, and expenses and ultimately distributing the property to the respective beneficiaries. The process is also referred to as administering an estate, and it generally occurs in the state where the decedent made his or her permanent home.

If someone dies without a will, state laws provide for the appointment of an administrator, usually next of kin, to oversee the settling of an estate. An administrator, executor, or other personal representative becomes the link between the decedent and the beneficiary. Harry has appointed Larry to fill this role for him. Larry technically gains authority to act when the will is admitted to probate and the court issues "letters of administration" or "letters testamentary" authorizing him to act. That is part of the probate process.

Since the personal representative steps into the shoes of the decedent, any property that was solely owned by Harry will be transferred into Larry's name during the period of administration. An important caveat here: Many states require an estate tax waiver before assets can be turned over to the personal representative. A separate waiver form for each asset of the estate is issued; it ensures that the state will be paid its share of taxes.

Even before letters are issued by the court, the sorting process can begin. Here, the bulk of the assets Harry left for Joan will not be caught in the probate process. The house is hers by virtue of the joint ownership, and the insurance and retirement benefits do not pass under the will. They pass to her because she was named on beneficiary designation forms.

Notifying the insurance company, the former employers, and the banks where the IRA funds are stashed is part of settling the estate. Usually a death certificate issued by the state or local health department, or the personal representative's letters from the court, must be produced for these entities to act. Other assets are handled similarly: checking and savings accounts, certificates of deposits, stocks, bonds, mutual funds, and cars.

What's the purpose of this fancy paperwork? Look at it this way. Let's say a good-for-nothing working with one of Harry's kids learns of the soon-to-be large inheritance and knows Harry's stocks are held by ZAP Brokerage. What's to stop him from showing up at the door and walking away with a bundle?

The whole process, that's what. With stock certificates, a transfer agent notified regarding a transfer of title will generally require proof of the executor's authority, and perhaps a tax waiver and/or death certificate as well. Only then will a new stock certificate be issued to Larry. The kids will have to wait until debts are settled, taxes paid, and settlement is complete before they get their legacies. ZAP Brokerage doesn't want to have to pay out twice, that is, once to the wrong people. That's why the red tape is in place.

All of the following steps are also part of settling the estate, marshaling the assets, and giving the personal representative control of the assets:

1. Getting a federal tax I.D. number for the estate, issued by the IRS.

2. Notifying the IRS of each personal representative acting for the estate.

3. Taking care of personal possessions, including paintings, jewelry, and other valuables.

4. Notifying the Social Security Administration of the decedent's death and determining whether survivors are entitled to any benefits.

5. Changing title to real property owned by the decedent either solely or as a joint owner.

6. Overseeing business interests, including settling business accounts and/or collecting wages, deferred compensation, or other benefits due.

After Larry gathers all of Harry's assets, what happens next? He safeguards them and makes sure that creditors are taken care of before assets are distributed. Harry's assets will pass free of federal estate tax because of the marital deduction and unified credit. However, there may still be state death taxes, and the cost of the probate and administration process itself. Once these liabilities, and any other creditors, are satisfied, the probate assets can be distributed.

Assets are first used to cover administrative expenses, funeral expenses, debts, and taxes. Thereafter, legacies are paid. So-called "specific bequests" come first. In Harry's case, he left a specific bequest of the car to Joan. Next "demonstrative legacies," such as the stock to Harry's kids, are paid. A demonstrative legacy is a specific amount from a specific source. The last legacy to be paid is the residuary estate. This may include the bank accounts if they were not specifically bequeathed under Harry's will.

Whether assets are subject to probate has nothing to do with their being tagged for tax purposes. For example, the insurance, employee benefits, and half the house will go into Harry's estate for tax purposes, even though they will not be subject to probate. If we assume Joan was Harry's girlfriend and not his spouse, his estate would be subject to estate tax, and assets which she receives may be needed to foot the tax bill. Accordingly, careful planning is required.

WHAT IS PROBATE?

Probate is just one part of settling the estate. Probate affects the property that is disposed of under a will. Each state has its own laws regarding what is necessary to have a valid will and how to prove it. This legal proceeding that passes on the validity of a will is probate.

The court proceeding is begun by filing what is generally called a "petition." It is filed with the appropriate state court that has jurisdiction over estates by the executor named in the will. It includes the name of the decedent and the names of the interested parties who should receive notice of the proceeding. Interested parties include those named in the will; those who would stand to benefit if there were no will; and beneficiaries named in prior wills. These individuals are given the opportunity to challenge the legitimacy of the will to be offered for probate.

When a will is offered for probate, the legal representative named in the will, that is, the executor, is appointed to represent the estate. If no will is offered, a family member (usually one authorized to step forward per state law) can petition to have a personal representative appointed. The personal representative's function is the same as that of an executor: to administer and dispose of the property of the decedent in accordance with state law. Before letters are issued, some states require a bond to be posted by the personal representative or executor. The need for a bond can be waived in the provision of a will that appoints a representative.

WHAT'S SO BAD ABOUT PROBATE?

Probably the worst thing about probate is the fact that in many states it costs far too much to comply with probate rules. The process of transferring title and liquidating assets involves fees to attorneys, accountants, and other fiduciaries, as well as to the system itself. Much detail work is involved and having a court oversee matters that may have been unnecessarily put in its lap is costly and frustrating. Then there's the length of time it takes to complete the process and the fact that the payment of legacies must be held up.

Some of this is unavoidable. If you leave a will, its validity must be passed on by a court. But a properly drafted will—one that does not spark disputes among disgruntled heirs and gives your executor broad powers to settle matters—should keep probate costs and delays manageable. Find out from a local lawyer how costly and time-consuming probate is in your state. It may well be that avoiding probate is not very important.

What kind of headaches can you avoid? Let's talk about some basics here. Assume that Harry and Joan have young children and have appointed Uncle Billy as guardian if they die. If that happens, the kids and their legacies become Uncle Billy's responsibility. Let's assume that Uncle Billy is a super guy, a great financial manager, and incredibly honest. Most courts won't care, because *all* guardians must keep records of even routine spending of the children's money. And Uncle Billy will have to petition the court for approval of all large expenses, perhaps even college tuition. Harry and Joan could have saved a lot of red tape by putting the money for their kids in trust and naming Uncle Billy as trustee.

Another possible headache can affect a closely held business. If you do not execute a buy-sell agreement, or make other plans that lay the groundwork for passing your business along, you will not only be leaving the nightmare of running your business to your executor, but all the dirty laundry as well. Whether the business is in fact being managed to the satisfaction of all the heirs may be aired in court, publicly and at your estate's expense.

Let's say that Harry and Joan agreed on all things in life, except how he ran the business and the children's place in it. He favored one son, Howie, neglected the hardworking second son Dan, and kept his daughter Pam on the payroll even though she never worked in the business. When Harry died, he still had not figured out what to do with the business. It passed under the residuary clause of his will.

Now his family, the executor, and the probate process are running the business. Joan still wants income from the business and Howie wants to be in charge and cut Dan and Pam off. Dan is resentful. Pam is willing to work but no one wants her in the business. And Larry, who is in fact a dentist, is stuck with decisions about a steel fabricating business that he knows nothing about.

Even if things run smoothly, a variety of experts, mostly attorneys and perhaps accountants and trustees as well, are needed. With these experts come fees, which may be significant. In this connection, fees are frequently quoted as a percentage of the probate estate. Some states prescribe executor's fees by statute. In others, fees are not set by statute and can be much higher. The fees associated with alternatives to probate, for example, creating living trusts, may in fact be a lot less. This should be checked out locally.

Another common complaint about probate is how long it takes to wind things up. In one sense, a lot of the detail work and winding up would occur and take time anyhow. The correspondence and documentation in connection with transferring title, closing accounts, etc. is time-consuming. However, probate adds a notification process, a layer of court approval, court papers, and accountings. It drags the court into situations where the court's involvement may have been unnecessary if other arrangements had been made. It can take between one and two years to wind up even modest estates, and this may be too long, particularly if the executor will not or cannot, because of the nature of the assets, make partial distributions.

The final reason for avoiding probate is publicity. Wills are public documents, and so are court proceedings concerning the will. Even if you're not expecting a will to be contested, you may not want your personal business in the public eye, no matter who's looking. You may not want the world to know the extent of your assets, or the favored status of certain beneficiaries under your will. A will is not the place to dispose of assets that you do not want in the public eye. Trusts can generally accomplish the same result without public scrutiny.

THE ALTERNATIVE TO PROBATE

The alternative to probate is to acquire and dispose of property that passes outside of your will. How do you do that? One way is to acquire assets that carry their own beneficiaries, such as insurance, jointly owned property that carries a right of survivorship, and retirement plan assets. The other way is to set up a trust that includes all the dispositive provisions you might otherwise put in your will.

Life insurance

As discussed in earlier sections, life insurance is handled in one of two ways. If you remain the owner, the proceeds will be included in your taxable estate, although your beneficiary will be the recipient of the proceeds. Since the proceeds are payable directly to your beneficiary, they are not included in your estate for probate purposes.

If Harry makes a provision in his will that his daughter Pam will receive his insurance proceeds, what happens? It will be of no force and effect unless Pam is named as the beneficiary of the policy. If Joan is the beneficiary, the provision in the will won't be operative.

Joint ownership of property

If you own property as a tenant by the entirety or as a joint tenant, the property will pass automatically, by operation of law, to your co-owner. If Harry and Joan own the house jointly as tenants by the entirety, Joan gets the house when Harry dies no matter what; Harry doesn't have to make a specific bequest of the house to Joan to achieve this result. It automatically becomes hers. Let's say Harry left his interest in the home to his son Dan. What happens? The bequest in the will is ineffective. Joan ends up with the house.

Joint ownership of property can exist for property other than real estate. Consider joint bank accounts, jointly owned government savings bonds, and other investments. If one owner dies, the other owner becomes the sole owner. The same is true for Series EE Savings Bonds and other investments. This is a convenient and common way to hold assets among family members. More complications arise outside the family context.

Retirement plan proceeds

These days, many people's first or second largest asset, along with their homes, may be retirement benefits paid by their employers. For married couples, a common form of payout from an employer-maintained retirement plan is a joint and survivor annuity. Or maybe it's a lump-sum distribution of assets you contributed to a profit sharing or 401(k) plan maintained by the employer. In either event, the death benefits payable from such plans are paid in accordance with your wishes as specified on a beneficiary designation form.

In some cases, you may have little choice but to name a surviving spouse as beneficiary. However, you may have the opportunity to name a living trust, or a trust created under a will, as the beneficiary of such proceeds. These proceeds are not included in your probate estate. Accordingly, there is room for maneuvering when selecting a beneficiary. Another advantage here, particularly if you have not yet retired, is that beneficiary designation forms are generally revocable until such time as you start receiving a payout from the plan. This gives you greater leeway to change your mind.

Living trusts

A living trust is created during your lifetime, but it can function much like a will. Unless it is irrevocable, it will not save you one dime in income or estate taxes. So what does it get you? It gets your assets out of probate.

Several aspects of the probate process are avoided by creating a living trust, as discussed in Chapter III. First, a disgruntled beneficiary has little recourse if he or she has objections to your trust provisions. The laws of some states require estate assets to be frozen for several months after death to give people a chance to come forward and challenge the will. Trust assets will not be frozen. With a living trust you can be assured there will be no interruption in the management of trust property at death. This can be very important.

Real life, real answers.

M arilyn Nowicki and Walter Robinson have been living together for a while and decide to buy a home as joint tenants with rights of survivorship. They are committed to each other and would want the survivor to end up with the house if something happened to one of them. As time marches on, Marilyn realizes that because of the payments she's made in connection with the house, she's been unable to accumulate other savings. It's all tied up in the house and with Walter. Walter has also been having some second thoughts. He too has been working to support the house. He thought he'd still be able to accumulate assets to pass on to his children from an earlier marriage, but this hasn't happened. If he died tomorrow, Marilyn would have the house and his kids would have no legacy.

Marilyn and Walter know some of the downsides of joint tenancy. You're tied in with the other person, perhaps to a greater degree than you care for, and you are unable to pass along the property to any other person under your will. Joint tenancy can be limiting; therefore, you should select your joint tenants very carefully.

It may sound reasonable to freeze estate assets pending a will challenge. But who provides for your family in the interim? Also, the purported goal of will contests is to overturn the will because the decedent allegedly lacked mental capacity. As a practical matter, though, many will contests are mounted because people feel they should have gotten more than they did. Settlements are common merely to avoid going forward with the costs of the lawsuit, and not necessarily because anyone raised a valid claim. This whole possibility can be avoided with a living trust.

Another problem associated with probate that can be avoided by a living trust concerns creditors. As part of the probate proceeding, creditors are given notice of your death and a right to come forward to submit claims. No notice of your death is required with respect to assets that will be distributed out of a living trust. Therefore, a living trust may protect more of your assets from the claims of creditors. Do not take this to the extreme however. Merely transferring assets to a trust to defraud creditors won't help you. In all likelihood, those types of transfers can be attacked in court.

FIRST THINGS FIRST

That's the last reminder of this book. You have been introduced to a number of techniques and strategies that can help you minimize taxes, probate problems, and other complications. But do not allow an "expert" to persuade you to use any of them unless they help you to accomplish your primary objectives. If you keep those objectives in mind throughout the planning process, you will end up with a will and an estate plan that give you peace of mind and a sense of both satisfaction and security.